# Good Health
# COOKBOOK

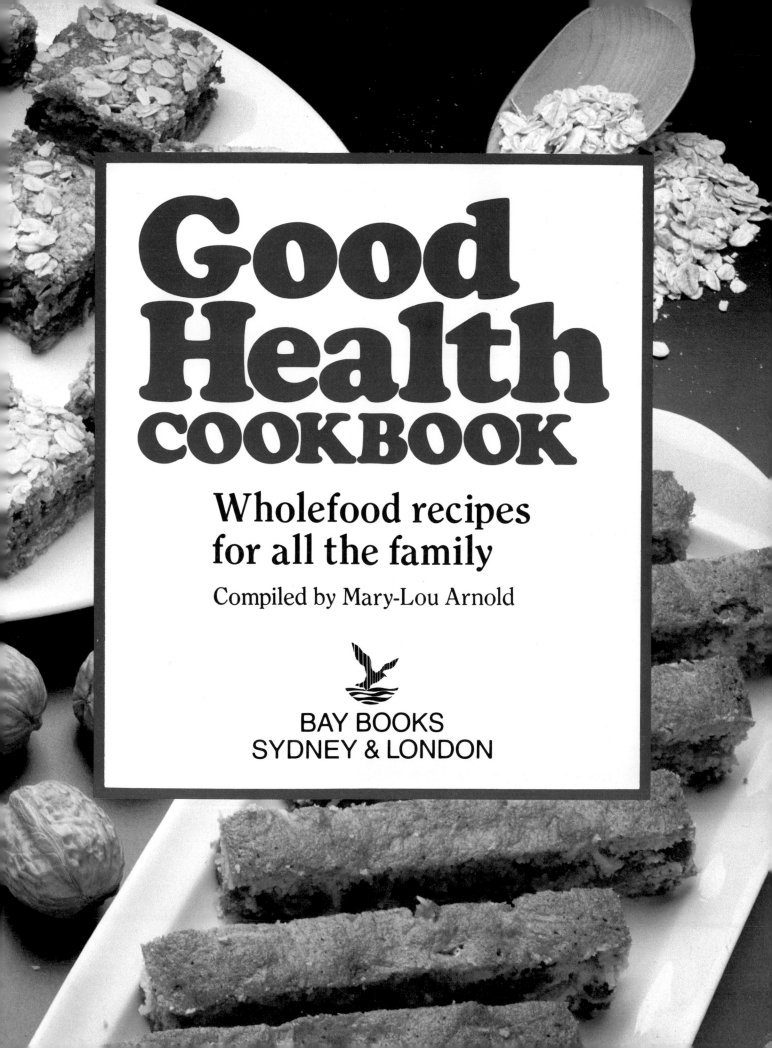

# Good Health COOKBOOK

## Wholefood recipes for all the family

Compiled by Mary-Lou Arnold

**BAY BOOKS**
**SYDNEY & LONDON**

Photography by
Ashley Barber

Food preparation and presentation by
Voula Kyprianou

Publisher: George Barber

Published in the
United Kingdom by
Angus & Robertson (U.K.) Ltd
16 Golden Square
London W1R 4BN

Copyright © Bay Books 1985

National Library of Australia
Card number and ISBN
0 85835 841 7

The publisher would like to thank the
following for their assistance during the
photography of this book: Ceramic
Crafts (Argyle Arts Centre), The Bay
Tree Kitchen Shop, Bendigo Pottery,
Bamix Australia, Outside In, Crown
Corning and Fred Pazzotti Tiles.

British readers please note the
following ingredients and their
equivalents:
- Eggplant — aubergine
- Zucchini — courgettes
- Thickened cream — double
  cream
- Cream — single cream

Bolivian Bean Stew *see Pulses and
Cereals chapter*

# CONTENTS

# INTRODUCTION

## How much do we know about the food we eat?

Almost all the foods we eat today have come under suspicion for causing some sort of disease or other at one time or another in our history. Even now, reports are so conflicting it is possible to become totally confused about what certain foods are supposed to be doing to our health. High blood pressure, cardiovascular disease, tooth decay, obesity and cancer have all been blamed on high intakes of foods containing excess amounts of salt, sugar and fats.

Is it possible to totally avoid all these ingredients? The answer is no. Salt, or sodium chloride, and sugar, or carbohydrates, occur naturally in varying amounts in virtually all foods and fats in dairy products, meat, poultry, some seafoods, nuts and seeds. Nor would we want to eliminate any of them from our diet as all three play important roles in the way our body works.

**Sodium chloride** is an essential mineral that acts with another mineral, potassium, to help regulate the water balance within the body. It also maintains health of the nervous, muscular, blood and lymph systems. Carbohydrates are the chief source of energy for all body functions and help regulate protein and fat metabolism. Fats are the most concentrated source of energy; they act as carriers for the fat soluble vitamins A, D, E and K, surround, protect and hold in place the kidneys, heart and liver, insulate the body and preserve body heat.

In fact, a daily intake of all five essential nutrients — carbohydrates, vitamins, minerals, protein and fat — is needed as they work with each other to keep the body functioning healthily.

**Protein** is a vital nutrient which provides the building blocks for the growth of cells and aids in the repair of damaged tissue. Proteins are composed of amino acids, the only

substance to provide the body with nitrogen, which is vital for life.

There are twenty-two amino acids which are essential for good health. For adults, eight of these must be supplied daily in food because the body cannot make them. They are lysine, leucine, isoleucine, valine, tryptophan, threonine, methionine and pheylananine. For children there is one additional essential amino acid, histidine, but the need for this is outgrown as the body develops and matures.

The other amino acids can be made in the body but, to ensure an adequate supply, they must also be present in our food. Often food containing the eight essential amino acids also contains some of the others. Food that supplies all of the eight amino acids in sufficient quantities is referred to as food of high biological value: meat, fish, poultry, eggs, milk and milk products.

**Carbohydrate** is a nutrient supplied by a large variety of foods and it has an important function. There are three types of carbohydrates: starches and sugars — which provide the body with energy, and cellulose — which is indigestible and provides the body with roughage. Nuts, legumes, starchy vegetables, grains and grain products are all sources of starch. Sweet fruit, vegetables, milk, honey and sugar provide the body with sugar. Whole grain cereals, vegetables and fruit are excellent sources of cellulose. Although fats provide a more concentrated source of energy for our bodies, carbohydrates are essential. Starches and sugars are more easily digested and metabolised by the body and so release energy more rapidly than fats.

**Fats** are needed for a number of reasons. They provide the body with essential fatty acids and fat soluble vitamins and they are the most concentrated source of energy. Fats

also have a satiety value: they create a feeling of satisfaction and fullness.

**Water** is another essential nutrient. An adequate amount of water must be consumed daily if the body is to function efficiently. About two thirds of our body weight is water and, as it is constantly lost by body functions, it needs to be replaced. Water provides a means of transport for all the nutrients in the body and carries dissolved or suspended substances into cells. It also transports waste from the body and helps to maintain the correct body temperature. Water aids digestion as well as keeping mucous membranes moist in the mouth, nose, eyes and digestive system.

It is only when excess amounts of any food or ingredient are eaten that the balance within the body systems is upset, the body reacts and we become ill. So the answer to whether various diseases can be blamed on excess intakes of salt, sugar and fat is yes. However, we can keep our bodies relatively free of any diet-related diseases if a well-balanced nourishing diet is followed.

Most of the recipes in *The Good Health Cook Book* are low in salt, sugar and fat. They are easy to prepare and, with few exceptions, are based on natural foods. Butter is a natural food, polyunsaturated margarine is not, but may be substituted if preferred. Instead of adding salt as seasoning, try kelp, a sea vegetable sold in powdered form, or a no-salt prepared seasoning mix. Cold-pressed oils retain their vitamin A and E content better than those oils extracted by heat, and may be preferred where oil is listed. These should be refrigerated.

*The Good Health Cook Book* recipes, which are divided into sensible categories for easy selection, cater for anyone who is interested in preparing and cooking natural and nutritious foods.

*Top*: Basic Wholemeal Bread, Irish Soda Bread and Granary Bread
*Bottom*: Rye Bread and Mixed Grain Loaf *see Breads chapter*

| FOOD GROUP | NUTRIENT | RECOMMENDED INTAKE |
|---|---|---|
| Bread and Cereals | Carbohydrates | 3 serves per day (depends on energy requirements)<br>1 serve = 1 piece bread, ½ cup cereal |
| Fruits and Vegetables | Vitamins<br>and<br>Minerals | At least 4 serves per day including 1 raw<br>1 serve = 1 piece fruit, ½ cup vegetable |
| Meat, Fish Poultry, Eggs, Nuts, Legumes | Protein | 2–3 serves per day<br>1 serve = 90 g |
| Milk and Milk Products | Protein | Children — 600 mL per day<br>Adolescents — 600 mL per day<br>Adults — 300 mL per day<br>Pregnant and lactating women — 900 mL per day<br>30 g cheese = 200 mL milk |
| Fats and Oils | Fat | 15–30 g per day (depends on energy requirements and other food eaten) |

# BREAKFASTS, BRUNCHES AND SNACKS

## Granola

350 g rolled oats
1 cup desiccated coconut
1½ cups chopped hazelnuts
4 cups sesame seeds
2 tablespoons wheatgerm
1 tablespoon brown sugar
100 mL oil
100 mL honey
1 teaspoon vanilla essence
1 cup sultanas

Mix together the oats, coconut, hazelnuts, sesame seeds, wheatgerm and sugar. Mix oil in a saucepan with honey and vanilla essence and stir over low heat until well combined. Stir the mixture into dry ingredients until well coated. Spread over a large baking tray and bake at 140°C for 35–45 minutes, stirring occasionally, until golden brown. Stir in sultanas and leave to cool. When cold and hard, break granola into small chunky pieces. Serve with yoghurt or milk.
    Makes about 1 kg granola

## Country Muesli

8 tablespoons rolled oats
3 tablespoons rolled barley
2 tablespoons rye flakes
1½ tablespoons buckwheat
¼ cup raw sugar
1 tablespoon sultanas
1 tablespoon raisins
2 tablespoons chopped dried apple
2 tablespoons chopped dried apricots
¼ cup chopped hazelnuts
¼ cup chopped walnuts

Mix all the ingredients together and store in an airtight container. Serve with milk, yoghurt, fresh fruit and honey. A 200 g packet of dried fruit medley can be substituted for the apples and apricots and unsalted mixed nuts for the hazelnuts and walnuts.
    Makes about 500 g muesli

## Mango Munch

1 large mango, diced
1 banana, sliced
1 tablespoon lemon juice
¾ cup granola cereal or toasted muesli
200 mL carton natural yoghurt

Sprinkle the lemon juice over banana slices. Divide mango between two serving dishes. Sprinkle with a little of the granola and cover with half the yoghurt. Spoon banana into dishes, cover with remaining yoghurt and top with remaining granola.
    Serves 2

Granola

# Cottage Cheese Pancakes

125 g cottage cheese, sieved
3 eggs, separated
1 tablespoon flour
1/8 teaspoon cinnamon
butter for frying

Blend egg yolks with cheese, flour and cinnamon. Whisk egg whites until stiff peaks form and fold gently into cheese mixture. Melt a little butter in frying pan. Drop batter by the large spoonful into pan and fry until golden brown on both sides, turning once. Serve immediately with honey, sour cream or yoghurt.
Serves 4

# Potato Farls

500 g potatoes, cooked and peeled
50 g butter
1 cup wholemeal flour
1 teaspoon bicarbonate of soda
1/2 teaspoon salt

Mash hot potatoes with the butter. Sift flour, soda and salt, add to potato and mix to a firm dough. Cut mixture in two and roll each piece into a circle, about 5 mm thick. Cut each circle into 4–6 wedges (or farls). Cook farls on a hot, greased griddle or frying pan until well-browned on the underside, then turn and finish cooking. Serve hot or cold, split and buttered.
Makes 8–12

# Cheese and Mushroom Savouries

1 cup grated Gruyère cheese
300 g button mushrooms, sliced
8 slices wholemeal or rye bread
150 g butter
4 eggs, beaten
1 clove garlic, crushed
parsley for garnish

Toast bread and lightly butter. Blend eggs and three-quarters cup cheese together. Melt remaining butter and gently fry mushrooms and garlic for 3 minutes, until soft. Stir in cheese mixture, season to taste and cook, stirring until eggs are scrambled. Divide mixture between toast. Sprinkle over remaining cheese and cook under grill until golden. Garnish with parsley and serve immediately.
Serves 4

# Apple, Cheese and Olive Savouries

3 red-skinned apples, cored and
  chopped
1½ cups grated cheese
4 stuffed olives, sliced
4 wholemeal bread rolls
50 g pâté
parsley for garnish

Cut thin slice off top of each roll and scoop out centre. Spoon apple into each and cover with pâté. Top with cheese and season to taste. Bake at 190°C for 20 minutes, until golden and bubbly. Garnish with olives and parsley.
Makes 4

Cottage Cheese Pancakes

Vegetable Tacos

# Vegetable Tacos

*1 packet taco shells*

## Filling

*2 tablespoons butter*
*2 tablespoons flour*
*1½ cups milk*
*2 hard boiled eggs, chopped*

*½ cup sliced mushrooms*
*½ cup grated carrot*
*2 tablespoons chopped shallots*
*1 cup finely shredded spinach*
*½ cup grated cheese*

Melt butter in saucepan, add flour, stir until smooth. Remove from heat and stir milk in gradually to make a smooth sauce. Cook until thickened. Add eggs and vegetables. Combine and cook 10 minutes.

Spoon mixture into taco shells and sprinkle over with cheese.

Makes 4

# Pizza Napoli

## Topping

*600 g tomatoes, peeled, seeded and chopped*
*2 tablespoons oil*
*2 teaspoons dried mixed herbs*
*250 g mozzarella cheese, sliced*
*2 cloves garlic, slivered*
*6 black olives*

Cook tomatoes and herbs in oil until soft. Spread over pizza base and decorate with cheese, garlic and olives. Bake at 200°C for 25–30 minutes.

Serves 2–3

# Basic Brown Pizza Dough

*1 teaspoon caster sugar*
*⅓ cup warm water*
*1 teaspoon dry yeast*
*½ cup wholewheat flour*
*½ cup plain flour*
*pinch salt*
*2 teaspoons lard*
*2 teaspoons oil*

Dissolve sugar in water, stir in yeast and set aside until frothy. Mix together flours and salt and rub in lard. Add yeast, liquid and oil and mix until sides of bowl are clean.

Knead dough on lightly floured surface. Clean bowl, lightly oil it and leave dough in it, covered, to rise until double in size. Knock back dough and knead until smooth. Put dough into round shape 23 cm in diameter. Brush with oil and leave for 15 minutes before baking. Top with Pizza Napoli (*see previous recipe*) or your own favourite pizza recipe.

Step 1. Add oil and yeast mixture to flours using a round-ended knife

Step 2. Knead dough on lightly floured surface

Step 3. Pat dough into pizza tray

Pizza Napoli

# Roast Beef Sandwiches

*12 slices cold roast beef*
*12 slices wholemeal bread*
*1 soft avocado*
*175 g cream cheese*
*30 g blue cheese*
*2 tablespoons chopped walnuts*
*½ teaspoon Worcestershire sauce*
*¼ teaspoon tabasco sauce*

Peel and pit avocado and mash with both cheeses until very smooth. Add walnuts, Worcestershire sauce and tabasco. Spread evenly on bread and top with roast beef. Decorate with a sprig of watercress, finely sliced onion rings or slice of tomato.
   Serves 6–12

Hint: Another way to prepare avocados; cut in half and hit seed with blade of sharp knife — so it holds the seed. Twist knife and pull to extract seed.

Roast Beef Sandwiches

# Pissaladière

## Quick Scone Dough

*2 cups self raising wholemeal flour*
*50 g butter*
*85 mL milk*

Rub butter into flour and mix in milk to make a firm dough. Turn dough onto lightly floured board and knead until there are no cracks. Pat out to round shape 23 cm in diameter. Place on greased baking sheet. Using forefinger and thumb, raise edge slightly by pinching the dough.

## Topping

*¼ cup oil*
*3 onions, sliced*
*250 g tomatoes, peeled and sliced*
*black pepper*
*250 g mozzarella cheese, sliced*

## Garnish

*50 g anchovy fillets, drained*
*20 stuffed green olives*

Fry onions in oil until soft, but not browned. Spread onions over top of dough, cover with tomato slices, sprinkle with pepper and top with cheese slices. Bake at 220°C for 20 minutes, until base browned and cheese bubbling. For extra taste add garnish of anchovy fillets and olives, and cook further 10 minutes.

Serves 2–3

Step 1. Stir milk into flour mixture

Step 2. Lightly press dough into dish

Step 3. Spread onions on top of dough

Pissaladière

# APPETISERS

## Hummus

*440 g can chick peas, drained*
*2 cloves garlic, crushed*
*½ teaspoon ground cumin*
*½ teaspoon salt*
*3 tablespoons sesame or olive oil*
*¼ cup lemon juice*
*1 tablespoon chopped coriander or parsley*

Pound chick peas until smooth and stir in garlic, cumin and salt. Add alternate tablespoons of oil and lemon juice, stirring well after each addition, until mixture forms a smooth, thick paste. Transfer to serving dish, chill and garnish with a sprig of coriander or parsley.

Serve with pitta bread and raw vegetable sticks.
Serves 4

Hint: All ingredients can be put in a blender or food processor and blended until smooth.

## Taramasalata

*2 slices stale wholemeal bread*
*75 g smoked cod's roe*
*1 clove garlic, crushed*
*good pinch cayenne pepper*
*1–2 lemons, juiced*
*paprika*
*150 mL oil*

Remove crusts from bread and soak slices in a little water. Remove skins from cod's roe and pound to a smooth paste. Squeeze bread dry and add to roe with garlic and cayenne pepper. Continue to pound mixture until it is really smooth. Gradually stir in lemon juice and oil and beat vigorously.

Transfer to serving dish, sprinkle with paprika and serve with toast.
Serves 4

Hint: All ingredients can be put in a blender or food processor and blended until smooth.

## Eggplant Dip

*1 large eggplant*
*1 onion, chopped*
*1 clove garlic, crushed*
*1 tablespoon chopped parsley*
*½ lemon, juiced*
*250 g cream cheese*

Prick eggplant with fork and bake at 190°C for 45 minutes, until very soft. Cool. Cut in half and scoop out flesh. When cool, blend flesh with remaining ingredients and season to taste. Spoon into dip bowl and serve with vegetable sticks.
Serves 6

## Cucumber and Grape Mould

*1 large cucumber, peeled and thinly sliced*
*500 g seedless grapes, halved*
*450 mL water*
*1 packet lemon jelly*
*5 tablespoons lemon juice*
*3 tablespoons orange juice*
*1 tablespoon grated onion*
*⅛ teaspoon cayenne pepper*

### Marinade

*3 tablespoons olive oil*
*1 tablespoon wine vinegar*
*¼ teaspoon mustard*
*¼ teaspoon freshly ground black pepper*
*¼ teaspoon powdered kelp or ground sea salt*

Thoroughly mix marinade ingredients and marinate cucumber and grapes for 30 minutes. Heat 150 mL water to near boiling and stir in jelly until dissolved. Add remaining water, lemon and orange juices, onion and cayenne pepper and chill until almost setting.

Drain cucumber and grapes well and reserve a few for garnish. Stir remainder into jelly. Pour into 1.5 litre mould and chill until set. Dip mould into hot water and turn out onto serving plate. Fill centre with reserved cucumber and grapes.
Serves 6–8

Taramasalata

# Lentil Spread

250 g lentils
400 mL water
25 g butter
1 onion, finely chopped
3–4 teaspoons curry powder
3 tablespoons tomato paste
1 teaspoon lemon juice

Rinse and drain lentils. Bring to boil in water and simmer over low heat for 30 minutes until soft and mushy. Mash with a fork. Fry onion in butter until soft but not brown. Stir in curry powder and fry for 1–2 minutes. Add lentils, tomato paste and lemon juice and mix to a smooth paste. Season to taste.

Spoon into serving dish and cool. Decorate with twist of lemon and serve with pitta bread or vegetable sticks.

Serves 6–8

Lentil Spread

# Wholemeal Salad Tartlets

## Pastry

*125 g plain flour*
*125 g wholemeal flour*
*1 tablespoon chopped herbs*
*125 g butter*
*1 egg yolk*
*2 tablespoons lemon juice*
*salt and pepper*
*iced water*

Place flours and herbs in bowl and rub in butter. Add egg yolk, then lemon juice, salt, pepper and enough water to form dough. Wrap in plastic and place in refrigerator for 20 minutes. Take out and knead on a lightly floured board until smooth. Roll pastry to ½ cm thickness and cut out with 8 cm cutter. Place in patty tins and bake 10 minutes at 200°C. Cool.

## Filling

*½ cup asparagus cuts*
*¼ cup steamed peas*
*1 cup chopped tomatoes*
*¼ cup chopped celery*
*2 tablespoons chopped chives*
*¼ cup grated carrot*
*¼ cup corn kernels*
*natural yoghurt*

Combine all vegetables and stir in enough yoghurt to hold filling together. Spoon into baked pastry shells and chill thoroughly before serving.
Makes 12

Step 1. Roll out pastry and place in patty tins

Step 2. Stir in enough yoghurt to hold filling together

Step 3. Spoon filling into baked pastry shells

Wholemeal Salad Tartlets

# Roquefort Mousse

2 tablespoons gelatine
250 mL cream
3 eggs, separated
300 g Roquefort or Danish blue cheese
2 tablespoons chopped chives
50 mL cream

Tie a double band of greaseproof paper around each of six individual soufflé dishes to come 2.5 cm above the rim.

Lightly oil inside of paper. Soften gelatine in the cream for 5 minutes. Stand mixture in a pan of hot water and stir until gelatine has completely dissolved.

Whisk egg yolks until pale, then gradually whisk in cream and gelatine mixture. Pour mixture into saucepan and stir over very low heat until thickened. Mash cheese and add

thickened mixture and chives. Leave to cool, then chill until beginning to set. Beat egg whites until peaks form. Beat cream until it is just thick. Fold cream and egg whites through the cheese mixture and divide between prepared soufflé dishes. Chill until set. Before serving, remove paper.
Serves 6

Step 1. Whisk egg yolks until pale, then add cream and gelatine mixture

Step 2. Mash cheese and add thickened mixture and chives

Step 3. Fold in cream and egg whites and pour into prepared soufflé dishes

# Caviar Mousse

2 × 50 g jars lump fish roe
1 tablespoon gelatine
4 tablespoons water
1 cup cream
2 tablespoons horseradish cream
2 hard boiled eggs, quartered
4 very thin slices lemon

Stir gelatine into water and dissolve over hot water in a pan. Cool. Whip cream, fold in horseradish cream and cooled gelatine. Reserve a little lump fish roe for decoration and carefully fold remainder into cream mixture. Spoon into individual soufflé dishes or 1 large one.

To serve, quickly dip dishes into hot water and turn out onto serving dishes. Garnish with reserved lump fish roe, egg and lemon slices and serve with toast.
Serves 4

# Fish and Pasta Appetisers

250 g smoked fish
175 g pasta shells
500 mL milk
3 tablespoons butter
3 tablespoons flour
¼ cup grated cheese
3 hard boiled eggs, chopped
50 g cooked, shelled prawns
squeeze lemon juice
pinch dry mustard
750 g spinach

Cook pasta shells in boiling salted water until just tender. Drain well. Poach fish gently in milk for 10 minutes until it starts to flake. Strain milk into a jug and make up to 500 mL with water. Flake fish, discarding skin and bones. Melt butter, stir in flour and cook for 1 minute. Gradually pour in milk, stirring rapidly. Simmer for 2 minutes, stirring. Stir in the cheese, pasta, fish, eggs, prawns. Season to

taste with lemon juice and mustard.
Wash spinach and remove white stalks. Cook in a little boiling water until tender. Squeeze dry and divide between 6 individual serving dishes and keep warm. Reheat sauce and spoon over spinach. Serve immediately.
Serves 6

Roquefort Mousse *top* and Caviar Mousse

# Stuffed Globe Artichokes

4 globe artichokes
4 lemon slices
2 tablespoons white vinegar
6 hard boiled eggs, chopped
3 shallots, chopped
5 tomatoes, peeled, seeded and
    chopped

Remove stems from artichokes and cut slice from top. Stand each on a slice of lemon in saucepan and cook in boiling salted water with vinegar for 15–20 minutes. Drain.

## Dressing

150 mL natural yoghurt
1 teaspoon honey
1 teaspoon Dijon mustard
1 tablespoon oil
1 lemon, juiced
1 tablespoon chopped parsley

Shake all ingredients together in a tight-lid jar until well blended. Mix with eggs, shallots and tomatoes. Gently open artichoke leaves to reveal centre hairy choke. Scoop this out with a teaspoon, discard. Spoon filling into centre.
    Serves 4

Step 1. Stand artichokes on slices of lemon and boil in salted water

Step 2. Add dressing to eggs, shallots and tomatoes

Step 3. Spoon filling into artichokes

# Camembert Creams

125 g Camembert cheese
15 g butter, melted
1 individual portion Petit Suisse cheese
3 tablespoons cream
1 teaspoon prepared French mustard
1 teaspoon finely chopped parsley

Remove rind from Camembert and mash the cheese with melted butter until smooth. Add the Petit Suisse and beat with a wooden spoon until well mixed.
    Lightly whip cream and stir into cheese mixture with mustard and parsley. Spoon into 4 small dishes and chill well. Garnish with parsley sprigs and serve with toast or vegetable sticks.
    Serves 4

Hint: Purchase only small amounts when buying spices or dried herbs as they can lose their potency after a few months. When using fresh herbs, double or triple the amount given for dried herbs.

# Carrot and Walnut Tidbits

500 g carrots
2 eggs
3 tablespoons wholemeal flour
salt and pepper
2 tablespoons parsley
¼ cup chopped onion
½ cup chopped walnuts
1 clove garlic
oil for frying
sesame seeds

Peel and chop carrots. Cook in small amount of water until tender. Drain. Process all ingredients, except oil and sesame seeds, in a blender until mixed to a paste. Chill. Form into small balls and roll in sesame seeds. Fry until golden in a little oil. Serve warm.
    Makes 24

# Brinjal Bhurta

*2–3 eggplants*
*oil*
*3 tablespoons very finely minced onion*
*2 tablespoons desiccated coconut*
*salt*
*pinch chilli powder*
*200 mL carton natural yoghurt*

Paint eggplants lightly with oil and bake at 180°C for 20–30 minutes, until soft. Allow to cool, cut in half. Scoop out flesh and mash with remaining ingredients, seasoning to taste. Chill before serving as a curry accompaniment or appetiser with pitta bread or vegetable sticks.

# Berry Ambrosia

*1 rockmelon or honeydew melon*
*175 g berries*

Cut slice from top of melon, remove seeds. With melon baller, scoop out flesh. Return melon to shell with berries of your choice.

## Dressing

*2 teaspoons French mustard*
*1 teaspoon lemon juice*
*¼ teaspoon vanilla essence*
*6 tablespoons honey*
*150 mL mayonnaise*
*150 mL cream*

Blend mustard with lemon juice and vanilla, stir in honey, mayonnaise and cream. Serve separately.
  Serves 6

Berry Ambrosia

# SOUPS

## Minestrone al Povero

⅓ cup cannellini or any small white
   beans
⅓ cup blue boiling peas
9 cups chicken or vegetable stock
1 large stick celery, chopped
1 large onion, sliced
2 medium carrots, sliced
2 tomatoes, peeled and quartered
½ cup any leafy green vegetable,
   sliced
1 teaspoon dried basil and/or oregano

½ cup brown long grain rice, or
   spaghetti
⅓ cup sharp cheese, grated
parsley for garnish

Soak beans and peas together in 3 cups of stock. Beans should be white and plump, peas green and plump. Discard any that are hard, brown or wrinkled. Add stock, beans and peas to remaining stock with celery, onion and carrots. Simmer for 1–2 hours until beans and peas are tender. Add tomatoes, leafy vegetable and basil and season to taste. Cook for 10 minutes. Add brown rice or spaghetti and cook 10–15 minutes until rice or spaghetti is tender. Serve with grated cheese and garnish with parsley.
   Serves 6

## Basic Light Vegetable Stock

2 large onions
4 sticks celery
4 medium carrots
2 medium parsnips
½ cup chopped parsley
3 teaspoons rock or sea salt
2 teaspoons white peppercorns
3 bay leaves
3 L water

Peel and chop onions roughly. Wash and chop celery, carrots and parsnips. Place all vegetables in a large saucepan and add salt, pepper, parsley and bay leaves. Pour in water, cover saucepan and simmer for at least 2 hours. Strain stock before use.
   Makes 1.5–2 L

## Basic Dark Vegetable Stock

2 large onions
2 tablespoons butter
4 sticks celery
4 medium carrots
2 medium parsnips
½ cup chopped parsley
2 teaspoons black peppercorns
3 teaspoons rock or sea salt
3 bay leaves
3 L water

Peel and chop onions roughly. Melt butter in large saucepan and fry onion until very brown. While onions are cooking, wash and roughly chop celery, carrots, and parsnips. Add to onions and stir well. Add all remaining ingredients to saucepan, cover and simmer for at least 2 hours. Strain stock before use.
   Makes 1.5–2 L

Minestrone al Povero

# Chinese Green Soup

1 tablespoon oil
½ teaspoon grated ginger
1 clove garlic, crushed
5 cups hot chicken or vegetable stock
1 cup rice
750 g Chinese cabbage, finely
    shredded

6 shallots, finely chopped
1 tablespoon dry sherry
½ teaspoon sesame oil

Heat oil in a saucepan and fry ginger
and garlic 1 minute. Pour in hot stock
and rice. Simmer 15 minutes or until
rice is just tender. Add cabbage and
shallots, simmer 5 minutes. Stir in
sherry and sesame oil.
    Serves 4–6

Step 1. Fry ginger and garlic

Step 2. Add rice and hot stock

Step 3. Add sesame oil and sherry

# Three-Bean Pasta Soup

⅔ cup dried red kidney beans
⅔ cup dried haricot beans
2 onions, sliced
2 tablespoons oil
2 tablespoons tomato paste
4 cups chicken or vegetable stock
175 g frozen broad beans, thawed
125 g mushrooms, sliced
125 g pasta rings

Soak the red kidney beans and haricot
beans in water overnight. Bring to boil
and simmer 1–1½ hours until tender.
Drain. Fry onion in the oil in a large
saucepan until soft but not brown. Stir
in tomato paste, stock and seasoning to
taste and simmer for 5 minutes. Add
the broad beans, mushrooms and pasta
to the pan and simmer for 10 minutes.
Add cooked beans and simmer for 2–3
minutes to heat through.
    Serves 6

Chinese Green Soup garnished with
capsicum

# Carrot and Orange Soup

*750 g carrots, sliced*
*1 onion, chopped*
*2 sticks celery, chopped*
*4 cups chicken or vegetable stock*
*1 bay leaf*
*1 tablespoon cornflour*
*grated rind and juice of 1 orange*
*good pinch nutmeg*
*¼ cup cream*

Place vegetables in a pan with the stock and bay leaf, cover and simmer for 20 minutes, until the vegetables are tender. Purée vegetables in an electric blender or push through a sieve. Blend cornflour with a little of the soup. Return the puréed vegetables to the soup with the blended cornflour, orange rind and juice, nutmeg and season to taste. Bring to the boil and simmer for 3 minutes, stirring. Pour soup into a serving bowl and decorate with a swirl of cream.
   Serves 6

Hint: To cook the soup in a pressure cooker, place vegetables with 1¼ cups of the stock and the bay leaf, bring to 6.75 kg pressure and cook 5 minutes. Reduce pressure under cold water, then add remaining stock.

# Buttermilk Soup

*3 cups buttermilk*
*1 small cucumber*
*salt*
*3 cups basic light stock (see recipe)*
*1 teaspoon French mustard*
*2 tablespoons minced celery*
*2 teaspoons chopped chives*
*2 teaspoons chopped fresh dill*
*2 teaspoons chopped parsley*

Peel and dice cucumber very finely. Sprinkle with salt and allow to stand 30 minutes. Rinse in cold water to remove excess salt. Mix all ingredients in large bowl and chill thoroughly.
   Serves 4–6

**Carrot and Orange Soup garnished with chives**

# Borscht

4 beetroots
5 cups water or stock
4 teaspoons yeast or vegetable extract
1–2 tablespoons lemon juice
2 tablespoons sour cream or yoghurt

Wash, peel and chop beetroots finely. Boil in water or stock for about 20 minutes or until tender. Purée in electric blender or push through a sieve, return to saucepan. Add yeast extract, lemon juice and season to taste. Reheat. Pour into a serving bowl and swirl in the sour cream or yoghurt.
   Serves 6

# Yoghurt and Cucumber Soup

500 mL carton yoghurt
1 cucumber, peeled, seeded and diced
2 cups chicken or vegetable stock
2 cloves garlic, crushed
½ lemon juiced
½–1 tablespoon finely chopped
   coriander
1 cup iced water
4–6 very thin slices lemon
2 tablespoons chopped walnuts

Cook cucumber in stock until just tender. Leave in refrigerator till cold. Mix garlic with yoghurt and lemon juice. Stir in coriander, chilled cucumber and stock. Pour in iced water and mix well. Serve topped with lemon slices and sprinkle with chopped walnuts.
   Serves 4–6

Yoghurt and Cucumber Soup

Step 1. Cook cucumber in stock until tender

Step 2. Stir in yoghurt mixture and chopped coriander

Step 3. Add iced water and mix well

28

# Watercress and Vermicelli Soup

75 g watercress
2 onions, sliced
1 L chicken stock
75 g vermicelli
2 hard boiled eggs, chopped
grated cheese

Wash watercress thoroughly. Discard stalks. Place watercress, onion and stock in a pan and simmer for 15 minutes. Add vermicelli and simmer for 2 minutes. Pour into serving dish and garnish with eggs and cheese.
Serves 4–6

# Fresh Tomato Soup

25 g butter
1 onion, thinly sliced
1 carrot, thinly sliced
1 tablespoon flour
750 g tomatoes, peeled and quartered
3 cups chicken or vegetable stock
1 bay leaf
pinch ground mace

Melt butter in a large pan, add onion and carrot, cover and cook over low heat for 5–10 minutes. Remove pan from heat and stir in flour. Add tomatoes, stock, bay leaf, mace and season to taste. Bring to boil, cover and simmer for 20–30 minutes. Purée the soup either in an electric food blender or by pressing through a sieve and return to the rinsed out pan. Reheat before serving.
Serves 6

Fresh Tomato Soup

# Country Harvest Soup

60 g whole wheat grain
50 g butter
1 small onion, finely chopped
125 g walnuts
2½ cups chicken or vegetable stock
1 bouquet garni
1 tablespoon flour
¼ teaspoon dry mustard
125 g cheddar cheese, grated
2 tablespoons cream (optional)

Soak wheat in boiling water for 1 hour. Melt half the butter in a large saucepan and fry the onion until soft but not brown. Grind walnuts on a board with a rolling pin. Drain wheat and add to the pan with the walnuts, stock and bouquet garni. Bring to the boil, cover and simmer for about 1 hour, until the wheat is tender. Melt remaining butter in a separate pan, stir in flour and mustard and cook for 2 minutes, stirring continuously. Remove from the heat and gradually add milk, stirring continuously. Slowly bring to the boil and simmer for 3 minutes, stirring continuously. Add the sauce to the wheat mixture with the grated cheese and season to taste. Heat gently, without boiling. Stir in cream just before serving.

Serves 6

# Lentil Soup

250 g brown lentils
1 onion, finely chopped
1 clove garlic, crushed
2 tablespoons parsley, finely chopped
2 tablespoons oil
2 large tomatoes, peeled and seeded
2 tablespoons wine vinegar (optional)

Soak lentils in water for an hour. Simmer 1 hour. Lightly fry onion, garlic and parsley in oil until onion is soft but not brown. Add tomatoes and fry for 5 minutes. Pour into lentils and reheat before serving. Vinegar gives a pleasant sharp taste if liked.

Serves 4–6

# Bean and Pea Soup

¼ cup red kidney beans
¼ cup lima beans
¼ cup yellow split peas
¼ cup chick peas
6 cups basic light stock (see recipe)
1 bay leaf
2 tablespoons oil
½ cup chopped onions
½ cup chopped red capsicum
¼ cup chopped celery

¼ cup chopped carrots
1 tablespoon chopped parsley
1 clove garlic, crushed
4 cups basic dark stock (see recipe)
1 bay leaf
⅛ teaspoon marjoram
⅛ teaspoon basil
½ cup tomatoes, peeled and chopped

Soak beans and peas overnight in light stock. Add bay leaf, bring to boil and simmer over low heat for 1 hour, until tender. Cook onion, capsicum, celery, carrots, parsley and garlic in oil for 5 minutes. Pour in dark stock and simmer until vegetables are tender. Add beans and peas and all remaining ingredients. Simmer 20 minutes. Remove bay leaves before serving.

Serves 6–8

Step 1. Fry onion, capsicum, celery, carrots, parsley and garlic

Step 2. Add stock and simmer until tender

Step 3. Add remaining ingredients

Bean and Pea Soup

# SALADS

## Kiwi and Cashew Salad

4 kiwi fruit
¼ cup cashews
few lettuce leaves
2 oranges
6 radishes
100 g mushrooms
small cucumber
2 sticks celery
vinaigrette dressing

Tear lettuce into pieces. Peel and slice kiwi fruit. Peel and segment oranges. Thinly slice radishes, mushrooms, cucumber and celery. Toss all prepared ingredients in a salad bowl with nuts and vinaigrette dressing.
   Serves 4

## Mixed Bean Salad

½ cup red kidney beans
½ cup black-eyed beans
½ cup chick peas
½ cup butter beans

Soak beans overnight in water. Bring to the boil very slowly for about 30 minutes. Simmer over low heat for 40 minutes, until tender. Drain beans, rinse and cool.

### Dressing

4 tablespoons olive oil
2 tablespoons lemon juice
1 clove garlic, crushed
3 shallots, chopped
⅛ teaspoon dry mustard
chopped parsley

Put all ingredients except parsley in a jar and shake to mix well. Pour over cold beans and mix to coat well. Sprinkle with chopped parsley.
   Serves 4

Hint: Cook extra beans and store in refrigerator for up to 10 days. Use instead of canned beans or add to salads.

## Farmhouse Salad

350 g cream cheese
1 cup grated Cheddar cheese
¼ cup cream
¼ cup chopped red capsicum
¼ cup chopped shallots
¼ cup pine nuts
3 teaspoons lemon juice
¼ teaspoon salt
¼ teaspoon paprika

1 lettuce
3 tomatoes
1 tablespoon chopped chives

Beat cream cheese until smooth. Beat in Cheddar cheese and cream until blended. Stir in capsicum, shallot, pine nuts, lemon juice, salt and paprika. Spread mixture into a freezer tray and

chill until firm. Wash and shred lettuce. Wash and slice tomatoes. Place lettuce on a serving platter, top with tomatoes. Remove cheese from freezer and cut into cubes, place cubes on salad, sprinkle with chives and serve.
   Serves 6

## Bean and Pasta Salad

175 g wholemeal macaroni, cooked
2 cups cooked chick peas
1 cup cooked broad beans
3 tablespoons olive oil
1 orange, juiced

1 teaspoon freshly ground black
  pepper
1 tablespoon chopped parsley or
  chives

Mix beans and pasta together in salad bowl. Shake remaining ingredients together in jar, pour over salad and toss.
   Serves 4

Kiwi and Cashew Salad

# Iced Summer Salad

*1 peach*
*1 banana*
*75 g strawberries*
*2 teaspoons sugar*
*225 g cream cheese*
*½ teaspoon ground ginger*
*2 tablespoons lemon juice*
*2 tablespoons cream, whipped*

*¼ cup chopped hazelnuts*
*shredded lettuce*
*vinaigrette dressing*

Peel peach and banana and hull strawberries. Dice fruit and sprinkle with sugar. Blend cream cheese with ginger, lemon juice, then fold in cream, fruit and nuts. Pour mixture into 4 individual moulds and freeze for 1–2 hours, until firm. Dip each mould into hot water and turn salad onto a bed of shredded lettuce. Serve immediately with vinaigrette dressing.

Serves 4

Step 1. Sprinkle diced fruit with sugar

Step 2. Fold in cream, nuts and fruit

Step 3. Spoon mixture into individual moulds

Iced Summer Salad

Fruit and Nut Salad

# Fruit and Nut Salad

2 grapefruits, segmented
2 oranges, segmented
1 cup chopped pineapple
1 large green apple, cubed
1 tablespoon lemon juice
½ cup stuffed olives
½ lettuce
¼ cup toasted pine nuts
¼ cup toasted almonds

¼ cup chopped walnuts
1 tablespoon olive oil
2 tablespoons vinegar
salt and pepper
1 tablespoon chopped chives

Combine pineapple, grapefruit and
orange segments and chill. Toss apple
in lemon juice to prevent browning and
add. Top with olives. Wash and shred
lettuce, place on serving platter. Spoon
fruit mixture over lettuce and sprinkle
with nuts. Combine oil, vinegar, salt,
pepper, chives and pour over salad just
before serving.
    Serves 6

# Whole Green Beans

500 g green beans
1 cm cube ginger, finely grated
1 teaspoon ground fenugreek
2 tablespoons finely chopped mint
1 teaspoon olive oil (optional)

Pour enough water into a saucepan to cover bottom and heat. Add ginger and fenugreek and heat. Add beans and mint and toss lightly. Cook over low heat until beans are just tender. Chill. The beans can be tossed in olive oil before serving.
Serves 6

# Melon, Tomato and Cucumber Salad

1 honeydew melon
1 cucumber
500 g tomatoes
50 g lemon balm leaves

Dice melon and cucumber. Cut tomatoes in halves then finely slice into half-moon shapes. Mix together in salad bowl. Finely chop lemon balm leaves and sprinkle over salad. Chill well.
Serves 4–6

# Spinach and Edam Salad

275 g spinach
175 g Edam cheese
2 carrots
1 red capsicum
2 shallots
4 radishes
75 g button mushrooms
3 tablespoons raisins
1 orange, juiced
1 lemon, juiced

Tear spinach leaves into pieces, dice cheese, cut carrots and capsicum into strips. Slice shallots, radishes and mushrooms. Place the prepared ingredients in a salad bowl with the raisins. Mix orange and lemon juice, pour over salad and toss lightly.
Serves 4

# Sicilian Fennel Salad

1 clove garlic, crushed
1 cucumber, peeled and sliced
1 onion, sliced
1 orange, peeled and sliced
4 tomatoes, sliced
1 bulb fennel, grated

## Dressing

1 tablespoon oil
2 tablespoons lemon juice
½ teaspoon chopped basil
freshly ground black pepper

Sprinkle garlic over salad platter. Layer vegetables and orange on platter and chill. Shake dressing in jar, pour over salad and toss lightly.
Serves 4

Spinach and Edam Salad

# Lebanese Salad

225 g burghul
225 g cooked, peeled prawn
225 g tomatoes, skinned, seeded and
    sliced
½ medium onion, grated
1 clove garlic, crushed
3 tablespoons parsley, finely chopped
1 tablespoon oil
1 teaspoon lemon rind, grated

2 tablespoons lemon juice
salt and freshly ground black pepper

Pour 350 mL boiling water over burghul and allow to stand 30 minutes. Drain. Combine all remaining ingredients and chill to serve.
    Serves 6

# Fruited Chicken Salad

1½–2 cups cooked chicken meat, diced
½ cup cooked brown long grain rice
2 grapefruits, peeled and segmented
2 carrots, julienned
2 teaspoons chopped onion
1 large ripe avocado
2 tablespoons lemon juice
1 tablespoon vinegar
1 tablespoon oil
lettuce or chinese cabbage
watercress

Place rice, chicken, grapefruits, carrots and onion into salad bowl. Season and toss well. Peel and dice avocado and cover with lemon juice. Combine vinegar and oil and add to chicken mixture with avocado and lemon juice. Toss gently. Blend dressing ingredients together. Serve salad on bed of lettuce and garnish with watercress. Serve dressing separately.
    Serves 4

## Dressing

6 tablespoons mayonnaise
1 teaspoon curry powder

Step 1. Mix basic ingredients and marinate avocado

Step 3. Prepare separate salad dressing

Step 2. Add oil and vinegar mixture

Fruited Chicken Salad

# Macaroni and Zucchini Salad

250 g zucchini
salt
1 cup sliced mushrooms
1 cup cooked wholemeal macaroni
¾ cup thin cream
¼ cup crunchy peanut butter
½ cup mayonnaise
1 tablespoon honey
1 tablespoon white vinegar
2 tablespoons lemon juice
½ cup roasted peanuts

Wash and slice zucchini. Place on kitchen paper, sprinkle with salt and allow to stand 30 minutes. Rinse under cold water and pat dry. Combine zucchini, mushrooms and macaroni in salad bowl. Chill while preparing dressing. Place all remaining ingredients except peanuts in blender and whip until smooth but not too thick. Coat salad lightly with dressing. Chill well and serve garnished with toasted peanuts. Extra dressing will keep well in refrigerator.
Serves 6

Step 1. Sprinkle sliced zucchini with salt

Step 2. Combine zucchini, mushrooms and macaroni

Step 3. Coat salad lightly with dressing

Macaroni and Zucchini Salad

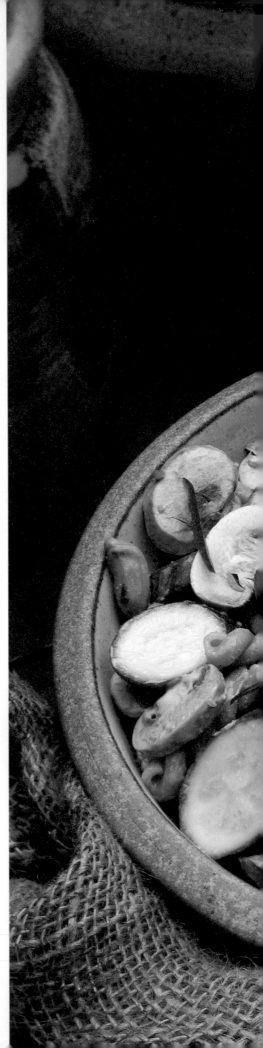

# PULSES AND CEREALS

## Hints for Using Beans

There is a wide difference of opinion on whether or not to soak dried beans and peas before cooking. Some cooks recommend an overnight soaking, others an hour or two. Some say soak in hot water, some say soak in cold water. Other cooks don't recommend any soaking at all. Some advocate draining the beans and peas before cooking, others suggest cooking in the water the pulses have been soaked in.

Pulses contain valuable nutrients including vitamins from the B group. These vitamins are water-soluble so if the beans are soaked in water and this water is then thrown out, these nutrients go down the drain. It should be sufficient to wash the pulses thoroughly and pick over and discard any that float or are discoloured. Pre-soaking shortens the cooking time, so if this is necessary by all means soak the beans in either hot or cold water. Bicarbonate of soda destroys nutrients and salt roughens the beans, so plain water is recommended.

Note: Cook extra beans and refrigerate or freeze for recipes requiring small amounts.

Hint: Dried beans and peas can be cooked in the pressure cooker. Soak overnight. Cook in 2.5–3.5 cm water and allow 15 minutes cooking time from when pressure develops.

# Bolivian Bean Stew

1 cup chick peas, skins removed
1 cup butter beans
1 cup lentils
chicken stock
1 green capsicum, roughly chopped
1 red capsicum, roughly chopped
4 sticks celery, thickly sliced
2 carrots, chopped
250 g tomatoes, peeled
310 g can corn kernels, drained
2 tablespoons tomato paste
1 bouquet garni

Soak beans and chick peas overnight. Drain and measure liquid, adding chicken stock to make up 600 mL. Place all ingredients in a saucepan and bring to boil very slowly — this should take about 30 minutes — then simmer for 45–60 minutes, until beans are tender. Remove bouquet garni and season to taste.
   Serves 6

Bolivian Bean Stew

# Haricot Bean Goulash

250 g haricot beans
4 tablespoons oil
2 cloves garlic, crushed
500 g onions, sliced
2 large green capsicums, sliced
375 g zucchini, sliced
1 kg tomatoes, peeled and quartered
4 tablespoons tomato paste
310 g can corn kernels, drained
1–2 tablespoons paprika
sour cream (optional)

Soak haricot beans overnight. Bring to the boil and simmer for 1 hour, until tender. Heat oil in large saucepan and fry garlic and onion until soft but not brown. Add capsicum and fry for 2 minutes, stir in zucchini and fry a further 2 minutes. Drain the cooked beans and add to the pan with the remaining ingredients. Season to taste.

Simmer, uncovered, for about 15 minutes until vegetables are soft. If liked, stir in a little sour cream before serving.
    Serves 6

# Barley Vegetable Casserole

⅔ cup pearl barley
2½ cups chicken stock
1 tablespoon oil
1 clove garlic, crushed
1 onion, chopped
2 sticks celery, chopped
2 carrots, finely diced
1 cup peas
2 tablespoons tomato paste

Soak barley overnight in stock. Bring to boil and simmer 1 hour. Drain barley and reserve liquid. Fry vegetables and garlic in the oil over low heat for 8 minutes, stirring so they won't brown. Add tomato paste and cook 1 minute. Add stock from cooked barley and simmer for 20 minutes until vegetables

are tender and liquid has almost evaporated. Add the barley and reheat.
    Serves 4

# Bean-filled Marrow

1 marrow

## Stuffing

1 onion
1 clove garlic
1 cup soaked soy beans
½ cup soaked red kidney beans
½ cup soft breadcrumbs
3 tablespoons tomato paste

1 cup grated Cheddar cheese
¼ teaspoon salt
¼ teaspoon cayenne

Prepare stuffing: peel and chop onion, place onion and all remaining ingredients in a blender and make a smooth mixture, do not purée. Cut marrow in half lengthwise and scoop out seeds. Fill cavities with stuffing and

place in baking dish. Pour water to a level of 2 cm in dish. Cover with foil and bake at 190°C until marrow is tender.
    Serves 2

Hint: Filling is also suitable for capsicums, zucchini or butternut pumpkin.

# Hungarian Bean and Vegetable Loaf

350 g borlotti beans
350 g soy beans
1 bay leaf
2 onions, finely chopped
4 cloves garlic
1 capsicum, seeded and diced
2 eggs, beaten
1 tablespoon oil
2 slices stale wholemeal bread,
    crumbled
1 tablespoon chopped parsley
500 g spinach
100 g roasted unsalted peanuts
100 g button mushrooms
1–2 chillies, seeded and chopped
1 small tin poivre vert (green
    peppercorns)
1–2 tablespoons paprika

Soak beans overnight in water to cover. Add bay leaf, bring to boil and simmer 1 hour until tender. When cooked, purée beans in blender with a little cooking liquid. Add onions, garlic and capsicum. Blend in eggs, oil, breadcrumbs and parsley. Season to taste. Remove white stalks from spinach and cook in a little water for 8–10 minutes until just tender. Purée spinach and press out excess liquid between two plates. Purée peanuts and mushrooms and add to spinach with chillies and poivre vert.

Place bean mixture on a floured board, flatten to thickness of 4 cm with a rolling pin. Top with spinach mixture in the centre and fold bean mixture over to form a loaf. Sprinkle liberally with paprika then arrange in a buttered ovenproof dish and bake at 190°C for 1 hour. Loaf may be served hot or cold.
Serves 6–8

Hint: Utilise blender or food processor to chop onions, parsley and breadcrumbs.

Step 1. Flatten bean mixture on greaseproof paper

Step 2. Place spinach mixture down the middle of the bean mixture

Step 3. Fold over bean mixture to form a loaf

# Cashew Nut Roast

1–2 tablespoons golden breadcrumbs
75 g butter
1 onion, finely chopped
100 g mushrooms, sliced
¼ teaspoon dried marjoram
125 g oatmeal
300 mL milk
1 egg, beaten
250 g raw unsalted cashew nuts, very
    finely chopped
a little oil

Lightly oil a 1 kg loaf tin and coat with breadcrumbs. Fry onion, mushrooms and herbs in butter for 2 minutes. Sprinkle in oatmeal, gradually add milk, stirring continuously. Cool slightly, then stir in egg, nuts and season to taste. Mixture should be a soft dropping consistency. Pour mixture into tin and smooth over surface. Bake at 180°C for 1¼ hours.
Serves 6

# Cannelloni Florentine

## Sauce

½ onion, finely chopped
1 clove garlic, crushed
2 tablespoons oil
500 g tomatoes, peeled and finely
    chopped
¼ green capsicum, finely chopped
1 bay leaf
⅛ teaspoon dried parsley
⅛ teaspoon dried oregano
⅛ teaspoon dried basil
⅓ cup water

Fry onion and garlic in oil until soft but
not brown. Add remaining ingredients,
season to taste and simmer for 30
minutes.

## Pancakes

1 cup wholemeal flour
1 egg
1 egg yolk
1 cup milk
15 g butter

Make a well in the flour, drop in egg
and egg yolk and pour in ¼ cup of the
milk. Using a fork, gradually work in
the flour adding the remaining milk, a
little at a time until batter is of a
pouring consistency. Add more milk or
water if necessary. Make 8 small
pancakes using more butter or oil to
grease the pan in between each
pancake if necessary.

## Filling

500 g spinach
½ cup Ricotta or cream cheese
¼ cup grated Parmesan cheese
⅛ teaspoon dried oregano
⅛ teaspoon dried basil

Remove the white stalk and chop
spinach leaves. Mix with the cheeses,
and herbs and season.
    Divide filling between pancakes, roll
them up and arrange in a well-buttered
shallow ovenproof dish. Dot with butter
and bake at 180°C for 10–15 minutes
until heated through. Spoon a little of
the sauce over and serve remaining
sauce separately.
    Serves 4

Step 1. Prepare sauce

Step 2. Fry pancakes

Step 3. Roll up filling in pancakes

Cannelloni Florentine

Ribbon Bean Bake

# Ribbon Bean Bake

*1 onion, chopped*
*1 clove garlic, finely chopped*
*1 tablespoon olive oil*
*¼ cup chopped celery*
*1 tablespoon chilli sauce*
*½ cup tomato purée*
*¼ cup tomato paste*
*¼ cup red wine*
*½ teaspoon salt*
*¼ teaspoon pepper*
*¼ teaspoon oregano*
*¼ teaspoon basil*
*½ cup cooked butter beans*
*½ cup cooked chick peas*

*½ cup cooked red kidney beans*
*1 cup cooked soy beans*
*½ cup cooked lima beans*
*250 g mozzarella cheese*
*250 g ricotta cheese*
*Parmesan cheese*

Heat oil and cook onion, garlic and celery 5 minutes. Add chilli sauce, tomato purée and paste, wine, salt, pepper, oregano and basil. Simmer 25 minutes. Combine all beans and peas in bowl. Slice mozzarella cheese thinly. Beat ricotta cheese in a bowl until smooth. Place one-third tomato sauce in bottom of medium-sized casserole. Spoon in one-third bean mixture and spread one-third ricotta cheese over beans. Place one-third mozzarella cheese on ricotta. Repeat until all ingredients used and sprinkle finished casserole with Parmesan cheese. Cover and bake 30 minutes at 190°C. Remove cover and bake 10 minutes more to brown.
　Serves 6

# Dhal

*500 g yellow lentils*
*1–2 tablespoons ghee or oil*
*2–3 onions, finely sliced*
*2–3 tomatoes, peeled and chopped*
*1 teaspoon chilli powder*
*2 teaspoons turmeric*
*1 teaspoon salt*
*2 tablespoons tomato paste*

Soak lentils in water to cover for 30 minutes. Fry onions in ghee until soft but not brown. Add tomatoes, chilli, turmeric and salt. Cook and stir for 5 minutes. Bring lentils to the boil, stir in onion mixture and simmer over low heat for 1 hour until thick and mushy. Stir in tomato paste.
　Serves 6

# Polentina

500 mL milk
¾ cup cornmeal
pinch mace
salt
pepper
2 egg yolks
50 g butter
2 tablespoons oil
1 onion, sliced
100 g mushrooms, sliced
1 green capsicum, sliced

1 chilli, seeded and finely chopped
½ cup canned baked beans in tomato
  sauce

Bring milk to the boil and sprinkle in the cornmeal. Simmer for 5 minutes, until thick. Season with mace and salt and pepper if liked. Remove from heat and stir in egg yolks and butter. Pour mixture into a greased shallow dish, level the surface and leave to cool.

When mixture is cold, turn out and cut into triangles. Heat oil and fry onion for 3 minutes. Add mushrooms, capsicum and chilli and fry for 3 minutes. Stir in baked beans and simmer for 4 minutes. Arrange cornmeal triangles around edge of an ovenproof dish and pour bean mixture in the middle. Bake at 200°C for 10 minutes. Serve immediately.
    Serves 4

# Rice Pie

1½ cups cooked rice
1 tablespoon butter
2 eggs
1 cup grated cheese
½ cup chopped onion
1 cup chopped celery
1 tablespoon oil
1 cup sliced zucchini
1 cup sliced mushroom
½ cup cream

2 eggs
salt and pepper
1 teaspoon chopped mint
1 sliced tomato

Add butter and lightly beaten eggs to rice while still hot. Press into 23 cm pie plate and sprinkle with half grated cheese. Fry onion and celery in oil until tender; place in pie, sprinkle remaining

cheese over. Layer zucchini and mushrooms into pie. Combine cream, eggs, salt, pepper, mint, and pour into pie. Bake at 190°C for 35 minutes or until pie is set. During last 5 minutes of cooking place slices of tomato on top for garnish.
    Serves 6

# Oriental Brown Rice

250 g long grain brown rice
3 tablespoons oil
16 shallots, chopped
1 clove garlic, crushed
2 tablespoons grated ginger
4 sticks celery, diced
150 g can water chestnuts, sliced
500 g bean sprouts
3 tablespoons chopped parsley
1 teaspoon dried oregano

½ teaspoon dried basil
½ cup sunflower seeds
½ cup honey
⅓ cup soy sauce
1 tablespoon lemon juice
310 g can mandarines, drained

Cook rice in boiling, salted water for about 45 minutes until tender. Drain well. Heat oil in a wok or large frying

pan and fry shallots, garlic and ginger for 1 minute. Add celery and cook for 1 minute. Add water chestnuts, bean sprouts and parsley and cook, stirring for 1 minute. Stir in herbs and sunflower seeds. Combine honey, soy sauce and lemon juice and stir into vegetables. Add rice and mandarines and heat through gently.
    Serves 6

Step 1. Stir fry shallots, garlic and ginger

Step 2. Add remaining vegetables

Step 3. Pour over honey, soy sauce and lemon

Oriental Brown Rice

# VEGETABLES AS A MAIN MEAL

## Braised Chinese Vegetables

¼ cup oil
1 teaspoon grated ginger
1 clove garlic, crushed
1 large onion, cut into eighths
1 carrot, sliced
1 stick celery, sliced
1 red capsicum, chopped
½ green capsicum, chopped
2 small zucchinis, sliced
200 g snow peas, strung
1 cup water chestnuts, halved
1 cup bamboo shoots, sliced

1 cup broccoli or cauliflower florets
½ cup chicken stock
1 tablespoon soy sauce
½ teaspoon sesame oil
½ teaspoon chilli sauce
3 tablespoons mung beans
shallot curls for garnishing

Heat oil in large frypan and add ginger and garlic. Cook until golden. Add onion pieces, carrots and celery and stir over high heat. Add capsicum, zucchini, snow peas, water chestnuts, bamboo shoots and broccoli and toss gently until heated through.

Lower heat, pour in stock, soy sauce, sesame oil and chilli sauce. Stir until combined. Cover and heat gently for 2 minutes or until vegetables are tender but still crisp. Remove lid, add mung beans and serve with rice, garnished with shallot curls.

Serves 4

## Normandy Corn Galettes

### For the pancakes

1¼ cups buckwheat flour
1 tablespoon wholemeal flour
1 egg
350 mL water
oil for frying

### Filling

50 g butter
½ cup flour
1½ cups milk

310 g can corn kernels, drained
½ cup grated cheese
1 large carrot, grated
½ teaspoon dried oregano
500 g spinach

Mix the flours, egg and water for pancakes and leave stand for 45 minutes. Melt butter, stir in flour and cook for 1 minute. Remove from heat and gradually stir in the milk. Bring to the boil and simmer for 2 minutes, stirring. Add corn, cheese, carrot, oregano and season to taste. Remove stalks from spinach and cook, covered, in a little water for 10 minutes. Keep warm. Make 12 small pancakes from the buckwheat batter. Keep warm. Reheat corn sauce. Divide spinach and corn sauce between pancakes and roll them up.

Serves 4–6

Braised Chinese Vegetables

# Zyldyk Casserole

250 g spinach
2 carrots, sliced
1 large zucchini, sliced
1 large onion, sliced
175 g cauliflower florets
175 g cabbage, shredded
25 g butter
1 tablespoon flour
750 mL skim milk
175 g Edam cheese, finely grated
2 teaspoons curry powder
2 slices bread, crumbed

Remove stalks from spinach and cook, covered, in a little water for 10 minutes. Place carrots, zucchini, onion, cauliflower and cabbage in saucepan and barely cover with water. Bring to boil, then drain, reserving 150 mL of the liquid. Place vegetables in an ovenproof dish and arrange spinach on top. Melt butter, stir in flour and cook for 1 minute. Gradually stir in reserved vegetable liquid and milk. Bring to boil and simmer for 2 minutes, stirring continuously.

Stir in 100 g of the cheese, curry powder and season to taste. Spoon over the vegetables. Combine remaining cheese with breadcrumbs and sprinkle over vegetables. Bake at 190°C for 30 minutes.

Serves 4

Step 1. Bring vegetables to the boil

Step 2. Place vegetables in ovenproof dish

Step 3. Pour sauce over vegetables

# Mughal Vegetables

3 tablespoons oil
2 onions, sliced
seeds from 6 cardamon pods
5 cm stick cinnamon, broken
2 tablespoons poppy seeds
¾ teaspoon chilli powder
¼ teaspoon ground cloves
250 g cauliflower florets
250 g zucchini, sliced
175 g carrots, sliced
175 g green beans, sliced
100 g mushrooms, sliced
⅓ cup desiccated coconut
¼ cup slivered almonds
¼ cup pistachio nuts (optional)
2 cups beef stock
150 mL sour cream
2 teaspoons lemon juice

Heat oil in a large saucepan and fry onion until soft but not brown. Add spices, vegetables, nuts and stock and season to taste. Bring to boil, cover and simmer for 15 minutes until vegetables are tender. Using a slotted spoon, transfer vegetables to a serving dish and keep warm. Add sour cream and lemon juice to liquid, reheat and spoon over vegetables.

Serves 4

Mughal Vegetables

Zyldyk Casserole

# Cabbage Cake

4 large green cabbage leaves to line a
 15 cm cake tin
3 cups chopped green vegetables,
 spinach, sorrel, Chinese cabbage,
 leeks, onions, spring onions (any
 variety of green vegetables in season
 may be used)
1 tablespoon herbs, tarragon, chives,
 parsley
1 egg
1 egg white
2 tablespoons plain yoghurt
2 tablespoons cottage cheese

Remove thick stalks of whole cabbage leaves and blanch 2–3 minutes in boiling salted water. Drain. Blanch green vegetables 2–3 minutes. Drain. Blanch onions and leeks 3–4 minutes. Drain. Line cake tin with cabbage leaves, tips to meet in centre, allowing base of leaves to hang over edge of tin, able to cover contents once filling has been added. Fill with blanched vegetables.

Fork egg and egg white together, add yoghurt, cream cheese, herbs and seasonings. Pour over filling and bring up cabbage leaves to close. Cover with foil and bake in baking dish half filled with water for 1 hour. Remove and allow to rest 15 minutes before turning out of cake tin. Slice and serve with fresh tomato sauce.
 Serves 4

# Loudou's Indian Vegetable Curry

2 teaspoons cumin
½ teaspoon turmeric
¼ teaspoon chilli powder
1 teaspoon salt
⅓ cup oil
2 large onions, chopped
2 cloves garlic, crushed
small piece ginger, grated
2 large tomatoes, peeled and chopped
4 potatoes, quartered
¼ head cauliflower, florets only
3–4 zucchini
½ eggplant
1 cup peas
½ cup water

Heat oil, stir in cumin, turmeric, chilli powder and salt. Add onions, garlic and ginger and fry, stirring until onions are soft but not brown. Add all vegetables except peas if frozen and fry, stirring, for 5 minutes. Add water, cover and simmer over low heat for 20 minutes. Add peas and simmer 5 minutes more. Most of the moisture should be absorbed during cooking period. Serve with boiled rice, brinjal bhurta (*see recipe*) and dhal (*see recipe*).
 Serves 4

Step 1. Fry onions, garlic and ginger with curry spices

Step 2. Add remaining vegetables except peas

Step 3. Add water and simmer over a low heat

# Vegetable Kebabs

## Marinade

*1 teaspoon garam masala*
*¼ teaspoon black pepper*
*⅛ teaspoon dried rosemary*
*1 tablespoon ground cumin*
*3 tablespoons sesame oil*
*½ lemon, juiced*

Mix all ingredients together in a jar and shake until well combined.

## Kebabs

*4 mushrooms — firm, whole*
*1 green or red pepper — square pieces*
*4 onions, small, whole*
*4 tomatoes, small, whole*
*½ eggplant, cubes approx. 2.5 cm square*
*1 banana, very firm but ripe chunks*
*250 g tofu, 2 cm squares*
*4 spinach leaves, rolled up into rolls approx. 2 cm thick*
*4 cauliflower florets*
*1 apple, square chunks*

Arrange choice of vegetables or fruit on skewers so that the cooking time of each is approximately the same. Brush over with marinade and either grill or bake on barbecue. Serve on bed of rice.
   Serves 4

Vegetable Kebabs

# Okra Casserole

*1 eggplant*
*2 carrots*
*2 potatoes*
*2 onions*
*¼ cup olive oil*
*4 zucchini*
*4 tomatoes*
*2 cups okra, canned or fresh*
*¼ cup chopped parsley*
*2 teaspoons oregano*
*salt and pepper*
*¼ teaspoon nutmeg*

Slice eggplant, sprinkle with salt and leave to stand 30 minutes. Peel carrots, potatoes and slice; place in boiling water and simmer 5 minutes. Drain and rinse under cold water. Peel and slice onions. Rinse eggplant and pat dry. Heat oil, fry onions until soft. Remove and fry eggplant until golden. Slice zucchini and tomatoes. Top and tail okra. In a deep casserole layer all vegetables, sprinkling each layer with a little parsley, oregano, salt and pepper and nutmeg. Cover casserole and bake at 190°C for 1 hour or until tender.
   Serves 6

Okra Casserole

# Baked Vegetable Ring

2 onions
2 cloves garlic
1 tablespoon oil
1 bunch spinach
2 cups cottage cheese
2 cups cooked soy beans
½ cup chopped walnuts
½ cup sultanas
¼ cup tomato paste
¼ cup grated carrot
¼ teaspoon dill
salt and pepper
1 tomato, sliced

Peel and chop onions and garlic, fry in oil until soft but not brown. Wash spinach and remove stalks. Steam until just tender. Chop finely and drain in a colander. Squeeze spinach to remove all excess liquid. Combine spinach with cooked onion and all remaining ingredients. Grease and line a ring tin. Place slices of tomato on base of dish. Cover with spinach mixture and press down firmly. Cover tin with foil and bake at 180°C for 45 minutes, removing foil after 25 minutes. If not firm after 45 minutes, bake 10 minutes more. Allow to stand 10 minutes before turning out onto serving plate. Fill centre with fresh tomato filling and serve.

## Fresh Tomato Filling

2 tomatoes
¼ cup chopped onion
1 tablespoon chopped mint
1 tablespoon lemon juice
⅛ teaspoon cayenne
⅛ teaspoon salt

Peel and chop tomatoes. Combine with all remaining ingredients and fill centre of vegetable ring.
Serves 6

# Spinach Soufflé

500 g spinach
1 tablespoon oil or ghee
1 teaspoon dried thyme
1 teaspoon dried oregano
250 g tofu
1 teaspoon kelp powder
½ teaspoon freshly ground black
    pepper
6 tablespoons water
4 egg whites

Remove white stalks, wash and chop spinach very finely by hand or in the food processor. Drain off excess liquid by pressing between two plates.

Sauté 5 minutes with thyme and oregano. Liquidise tofu with kelp and water in food processor or blender. Add pepper. Mix with spinach and leave to cool. Whisk egg whites until stiff peaks form. Gently fold through spinach mixture. Lightly oil a soufflé dish and fill with spinach mixture. Bake at 190°C for 30–35 minutes. Serve immediately.
Serves 4

# Eggplant and Potato Bake

2 large eggplants
salt
1 kg potatoes
1 tablespoon oil
2 large onions, sliced
1–1½ cups grated cheese

Slice eggplants, sprinkle with salt and leave to stand 30 minutes. Cook potatoes until just tender, peel and slice. Rinse eggplants and pat dry. Fry onion in oil until soft, but not brown. Arrange a layer of eggplants in a casserole, sprinkle lightly with cheese, cover with a layer of potatoes, top with onions and sprinkle over a little cheese.

Continue these layers, finishing with eggplants topped with cheese, season to taste. Cover dish and bake at 190°C for 1¼ hours, remove lid and bake for further 15 minutes, until golden brown.
Serves 4

# Carrots in Sour Cream

600 g carrots, thinly sliced
35 g butter
½ lemon, juiced
2 tablespoons sultanas
150 mL sour cream
⅛ teaspoon grated nutmeg
chopped parsley

Cook carrots gently in butter in covered saucepan for 20 minutes until tender. Shake saucepan occasionally to prevent sticking. Stir in lemon juice, sultanas and sour cream, season with nutmeg and garnish with parsley.
Serves 4

Step 1. Fry onions and garlic until soft

Step 2. Combine remaining ingredients

Step 3. Place slices of tomato on base of ring dish and spoon in mixture

Baked Vegetable Ring

# MEAT AND FISH

## Pork Goulash

750 g pork fillet, cubed
4 tablespoons paprika
2 tablespoons butter
1 large onion, sliced
1 red capsicum, sliced
1 green capsicum, sliced
5 tablespoons flour
200 mL chicken stock
150 g button mushrooms

8 tomatoes, peeled and chopped
1 cup sour cream
1 tablespoon chopped dill for garnish

Sprinkle pork with 2 tablespoons paprika. Brown meat in butter in frypan and drain. Sauté onions and capsicum until tender and remove. Stir in flour and remaining paprika. Cook for 2 minutes. Stir in stock and bring to boil. Place pork, sauce, mushrooms and tomatoes into saucepan. Cover and simmer for 45 minutes. Stir half the cream through the dish prior to serving. Garnish with a dollop of sour cream and a sprinkle of dill or chopped chives. Serve with boiled baby potatoes and any other green vegetable.
Serves 4

## Beef Cobbler

750 g chuck steak, cubed
¼ cup oil
1 onion, chopped
1 carrot, chopped
4 tablespoons flour
2 tablespoons tomato paste
300 mL beef stock
300 mL beer

1 clove garlic, crushed
⅛ teaspoon dried rosemary
1 tablespoon milk
1 tablespoon chopped parsley

Brown steak in oil. Add onion and carrot and cook 5 minutes. Stir in flour and cook 1 minute. Add tomato paste, stock, beer, garlic, rosemary, milk and chopped parsley and bring to the boil. Transfer to ovenproof dish, cover and bake at 150°C for 2 hours, until beef is tender.
Serves 6

## Eggplant Khoresh

1 large eggplant, sliced
¾ cup haricot beans, soaked overnight
2 carrots, sliced
2 onions, sliced
1 tablespoon oil
1 kg best end neck of mutton, cut in chunks
½ cup seasoned flour

450 mL beef stock
1 tablespoon tomato paste
2 sticks celery, chopped

Drain beans. Fry onions and carrots in oil until soft, but not brown. Remove with slotted spoon. Lightly coat lamb with seasoned flour and brown. Add all remaining ingredients, bring to the boil, cover and simmer for 2½ hours until meat and beans are tender. If possible, leave in refrigerator till cold to allow fat to set. Remove fat and reheat thoroughly before serving.
Serves 4–6

## Lamb and Nut Korma

750 g lean lamb, cut in bite-size pieces
50 g raw, unsalted cashew nuts
3 dried chillies
2 teaspoons ground coriander
1 teaspoon ground ginger
1 teaspoon ground cumin
½ teaspoon ground cinnamon
⅛ teaspoon ground cardamom
⅛ teaspoon ground cloves
2 cloves garlic, crushed
150 mL water

2 onions, chopped
50 g butter or ghee
150 mL natural yoghurt
grated rind ½ lemon
2 teaspoons lemon juice
½ teaspoon turmeric

Grind nuts and chillies together. If using food processor a little water may be needed. Mix coriander, ginger, cumin, cinnamon, cardamom, cloves and garlic together. Add nut mixture and mix with water to a smooth paste.
Fry onions in butter over low heat until soft but not brown. Stir in paste and yoghurt and fry until the oil separates. Add remaining ingredients. Bring to the boil, cover and simmer over low heat for 1 hour.
Serves 4

# Veal Parmigiana

4 large veal scallops
seasoning to taste
1 cup flour, sifted
½ teaspoon oregano
2 eggs, beaten
½ cup grated parmesan
1½ cups breadcrumbs
oil for frying
1 cup grated mozzarella

2 cups tomato sauce, fresh or canned
4 tablespoons snipped chives

Flatten scallops with meat mallet. Season each scallop and coat with flour. Combine oregano with egg and parmesan with the breadcrumbs. Dip each scallop into egg and coat with breadcrumbs. Heat oil and fry each scallop over high heat 1 minute each side. Remove from pan and place into a shallow casserole. Sprinkle each scallop with grated mozzarella and pour sauce over or on the crumbed veal scallops. Bake in a moderate oven for 10 minutes or until cheese melts. Serve sprinkled with chives and a side salad.
Serves 4

# Apollo Steak

## Sauce

1 lambs kidney, skinned, cored and
    sliced
25 g butter
1 large onion, sliced
2 tomatoes, peeled, seeded and
    chopped
1 green capsicum, seeded and chopped

150 mL red wine
150 mL beef stock
⅛ teaspoon oregano

Melt butter in saucepan and fry kidney and vegetables for 5 minutes, until tender. Add wine, stock, oregano and season to taste. Bring to boil and simmer for 5 minutes.

## Steak

4 sirloin or rump steaks
2 tablespoons oil

Fry steak in oil or cook under grill according to taste. Spoon sauce over and serve immediately.
Serves 4

# Provençale Chicken

8 chicken pieces
salt, pepper, cinnamon
¼ cup oil
1 clove garlic, crushed
1 bunch spring onions
1 green capsicum, cut in strips
200 g button mushrooms
4 large tomatoes, seeded and chopped
120 mL Chablis or other white wine
250 mL tomato purée
1 bouquet garni

seasonings
2 tablespoons parsley, chopped
16 black olives

Season chicken pieces with salt, pepper and cinnamon. Heat oil in frypan and brown chicken pieces. Remove from pan and drain on kitchen towel. Lightly sauté garlic, spring onions, capsicum and mushrooms. Remove and drain. Sauté tomato pieces then add wine.

Return vegetables to pan. Add tomato purée and bouquet garni and heat gently. Season sauce. Add chicken pieces to pan with sauce, heat, then remove bouquet garni. Arrange chicken on serving dish and pour sauce with vegetables over. Sprinkle with parsley and olives. Serve hot with buttered pasta.
Serves 4

Step 1. Lightly sauté garlic, spring onions, capsicum and mushrooms

Step 2. Sauté tomato pieces and add wine

Step 3. Mix all ingredients and heat through

Provençale Chicken

# Stir-fried Chicken

4 chicken breasts, cut into strips
2 teaspoons soy sauce
1 large onion, quartered
1 teaspoon grated ginger
1 clove garlic, crushed
2 sticks celery, sliced diagonally
1 red capsicum, sliced
1 small carrot, sliced/chopped
1 can baby corn
4 cups button mushrooms
2 teaspoons cornflour
200 mL chicken stock
4 stalks shallots

1 teaspoon soy sauce
1 teaspoon oyster sauce
1 teaspoon dry sherry
1 teaspoon honey
oil for frying

Sprinkle soy sauce over chicken strips. Cut, slice, chop all vegetables Chinese style. Heat oil in wok and gently fry chicken until cooked. Remove and drain. Heat oil in wok and quickly fry onion, ginger, garlic and celery over high heat. Add capsicum, carrot, baby corn, stirring continuously. Lower heat and stir in button mushrooms.

Blend cornflour with stock and stir into wok with chicken pieces and remaining ingredients. Cook until heated through. Serve with boiled noodles. Garnish with chopped coriander.

Serves 6

# Spicy Peanut Roast Chicken

1 × 1.5 kg chicken
1 teaspoon paprika
1 teaspoon ground ginger
1/8 teaspoon cayenne pepper
3 tablespoons oil
3 cups raw unsalted peanuts
125 g butter
3–4 slices wholemeal bread
2 tablespoons rum

Mix paprika, ginger, cayenne and oil well together. Grind 1 cup peanuts and add half resulting powder to oil and spice mixture. Coat chicken all over with nut mixture and bake at 180°C for 1½ hours until tender. Mix remaining ground peanuts with half the butter. Toast bread and spread with butter mixture. Place on a baking sheet and cook in oven 5–10 minutes, until topping is brown and bubbling. Fry remaining peanuts in rest of butter until pale golden. To serve, cut toast in half and arrange around chicken on hot serving dish. Sprinkle over the peanuts, heat rum carefully, pour over chicken and set alight.

Serves 6

# Gemfish with Peanut Sauce

1 kg gemfish fillets
2 tablespoons flour
25 g butter
2 tablespoons oil
2 tablespoons smooth peanut butter
1 tablespoon honey
1 tablespoon soy sauce
1 tablespoon vinegar
150 mL flat light beer
1/8 teaspoon chilli powder
½ cup raw unsalted peanuts
1 lemon

Skin fish and divide into four pieces. Coat lightly with flour. Fry first in oil and butter for 5 minutes each side. Boil remaining ingredients, except peanuts, until reduced by half. Add peanuts and simmer over low heat for 3 minutes.

Transfer fish to heated serving dish and spoon sauce over. Garnish with lemon wedges or cherries.

Serves 4

**Gemfish with Peanut Sauce**

Stir-fried Chicken

# Jewfish Fish Balls

500 g white fish
1 egg, beaten
75 g medium matzo meal
1 small onion, finely chopped
a little flour
250 g carrots, thinly sliced
450 mL fish stock
1 bay leaf

Mince fish and combine with egg, matzo meal and onion and season to taste. Roll mixture into 12 balls, using floured hands.

Arrange carrots and fish balls in shallow ovenproof dish. Pour stock over and add bay leaf. Cover and bake at 180°C for 1 hour. Remove bay leaf before serving.

Serves 4

# Curried Fish Risotto

750 g white fish, skinned and boned
2 tablespoons oil
1 large onion, chopped
1 tablespoon flour
1–2 tablespoons curry powder
550 mL chicken stock
1 cup long grain rice
1 green capsicum, sliced

1 small Granny Smith apple, peeled, cored and chopped
1 tablespoon sultanas

Fry onion in oil until soft, but not brown. Stir in flour and curry powder and cook 1 minute. Stir in stock, rice, capsicum, apple and sultanas, season to taste. Cover and simmer 15 minutes, stirring occasionally. Cut fish into bite-size pieces, add to curry and simmer for further 5 minutes, until rice and fish are cooked.

Serves 4

# Scallops and Prawns, St Jacques Orly

20 scallops
20 green king prawns
1 cup white wine
1 cup water
bouquet garni
seasonings
wholemeal flour
batter
2 cups oil
tartare sauce
lemon wedges
parsley

Clean scallops and peel prawns, removing veins. Heat wine with water and bouquet garni. Blanch seafood in liquid, remove and drain. Season seafood, coat with flour and dip into batter. Deep fry each piece until golden, drain. Serve hot with tartare sauce. Garnish with lemon wedges and/or parsley.

## Batter

2 cups wholemeal flour
2 cups milk
1 egg, separated
pinch salt
pinch cayenne pepper

Sift flour. Blend in milk and egg yolk, salt and cayenne pepper. Rest for 20 minutes. Beat egg white until stiff and fold into batter. Use to coat seafood.

## Tartare

1 cup mayonnaise
1 teaspoon capers, finely chopped
1 teaspoon chives
1 teaspoon French mustard

Combine all ingredients and serve chilled.

Serves 4

Step 1. Blanch seafood in wine mixture

Step 2. Dip seafood in flour and then batter

Step 3. Deep fry until golden

Scallops and Prawns, St Jacques Orly

# BREADS

Breadmaking with yeast takes time rather than special skills, time for the dough to prove or rise. A dough will rise in about 30 minutes in a warm place where the temperature is around 30°C. If left say on the kitchen table it can take up to 5 hours (or overnight if stored on the bottom shelf of the refrigerator). A dough that is allowed to rise slowly will produce a better quality bread that will remain fresh longer. If time is a factor, the proving or rising process can be hurried along by adding a little extra yeast and warming the flour and bowl.

When leaving the dough to prove, make sure it is not in a draught, in direct sunlight or close to direct heat. For a handy warm place, just turn on the oven before mixing the dough, then turn off and stand the bowl on a wooden board on the oven door.

*Hints for better breadmaking*

☐ Fresh yeast is cheaper than dried yeast and can usually be purchased at small bakeries, health food shops and speciality delicatessens. Well wrapped, it will keep up to 4 weeks in a refrigerator.

☐ Dried yeast is twice as strong as fresh yeast. Substitute 1 tablespoon (15 g) of dried yeast for 30 g fresh.

☐ A dough hook on an electric mixer may be used for the kneading process.

☐ For a lighter wholemeal bread, substitute white flour for some of the wholemeal flour.

☐ For a darker coloured loaf, add a little molasses.

☐ Leftover dough, well wrapped in plastic wrap or foil, can be stored in the refrigerator for up to 48 hours. When required leave at room temperature for 1 hour before shaping and proving.

☐ Heavy, earthenware flowerpots make ideal rustic moulds for baked bread. Before using for the first time, grease the flowerpot and bake it empty in a hot oven 2 or 3 times. This will prevent the dough from sticking to the sides.

☐ Try different toppings on your loaves. Sprinkle before baking with sesame, poppy or caraway seeds, cracked wheat or rock salt. Or mix together some finely chopped nuts with a little honey and paint over the loaf for the last 5 minutes of cooking time.

☐ Both dough and cooled, cooked loaves can be frozen. Wrap in foil or plastic bag and thaw at room temperature or overnight in the refrigerator. Shape dough and allow to rise again before baking.

☐ When using bicarbonate of soda or baking powder, cook immediately or bread will not rise.

☐ Fresh yeast may be frozen. Grate into flour or liquid without thawing.

☐ To freeze pizzas, cover dough with topping, wrap in plastic wrap or foil. To serve, unwrap and bake, without thawing at 200°C for 1 hour.

*Top*: Basic Wholemeal Bread, Irish Soda Bread and Granary Bread
*Bottom*: Rye Bread and Mixed Grain Loaf

71

# Basic Wholemeal Bread

40 g fresh yeast
1 teaspoon sugar
125 mL milk
500 g wholemeal flour
1 teaspoon salt
125 mL warm water
1 tablespoon oil
extra milk

Heat milk to blood temperature, add sugar and crumbled yeast. (If the milk is too warm it will kill the yeast; if it is too cool the yeast will not be activated. Set aside in a warm place until mixture is frothy. This should take about 10 minutes. Place flour and salt in a bowl. Combine warm water and oil, stir into flour. The oil helps keep the loaf fresh longer. Pour the frothy yeast mixture into bowl and combine to form a smooth dough. If mixture is too stiff or too dry add some more warm milk. It is better to have mixture slightly sticky at this stage because if it is too stiff the gas the yeast produces will not be able to escape and prove the dough. Yeast needs liquid in order to grow and develop.

Place dough in a warmed, lightly greased bowl and cover with a damp cloth. Put the bowl in a warm place and leave until dough has doubled in size. This is the process of proving and usually takes about 1 hour. If the dough does not appear to grow there are several possibilities: the dough may be either too cold or too hot, the yeast may be stale or it may have been killed earlier. If this occurs it is best to start again.

Turn dough out onto a lightly floured board and knead well. Kneading is necessary to develop the gluten, a wheat protein which is very elastic if worked with moisture and warmth. To knead, punch the dough into a round flat shape, bring part of the edge back into the centre, then push down and out towards the edge again. Turn dough around. Take another part of the edge and repeat the kneading process. Continue this for at least 10 minutes until the dough becomes smooth and elastic. Test dough by gently pressing with a dry finger; if it springs back, it is ready.

Shape dough into 2 loaves of equal size and place in oiled bread tins. Avoid creases and folds on the surface. Tin should be about two thirds full; if fuller, the dough may overflow; if less than half full, a very dense loaf may result. Cover tins with a damp cloth and set in a warm place until the dough has doubled in size or reaches the top of the tin. This should take about 30–45 minutes.

Bake loaves at 200°C for 20 minutes, reduce heat to 180°C and bake a further 30–40 minutes. To test, remove loaf from tin and tap gently on base. If it sound hollow, the loaf is cooked. Place bread on a wire rack, cover with a dry, clean cloth and allow to cool. When freezing bread, be sure it is completely cold before wrapping and placing in freezer.

# Spoonbread

475 mL milk
1 cup cornmeal
½ teaspoon salt
½ teaspoon baking powder
2 teaspoons brown sugar
15 g butter
2 eggs, separated

Heat 300 mL of the milk until bubbles form, stir in cornmeal and cook 1–2 minutes. Remove from heat and combine with salt, baking powder, brown sugar, butter, egg yolks and remaining milk. Whisk egg whites until stiff peaks form and gently fold into cornmeal mixture. Pour into buttered 1 litre soufflé dish. Bake at 180°C 40–45 minutes until golden. Serve from dish.

Serves 4

# Irish Soda Bread

2 cups wholemeal flour
2¼ cups flour
1 teaspoon salt
2 teaspoons bicarbonate of soda
300 mL buttermilk

Sift flours, salt and bicarbonate of soda and stir in buttermilk a little at a time and beat until dough is firm and leaves sides of bowl clean. Turn onto floured surface and knead until smooth. Shape into flattish round loaf 20 cm in diameter. Place on greased baking tray and using sharp knife or razor blade, cut a deep cross in the top. Bake at 220°C 30–35 minutes.

# Dilled Oat Bread

1 cup rolled oats
2 tablespoons dill seeds
¼ cup brown sugar
½ cup warm water
2 tablespoons dried yeast
1 small onion, chopped
2 cups cottage cheese
3 tablespoons butter
2 teaspoons salt
2 eggs
2 cups buckwheat flour
1½ cups wholemeal flour

Dissolve 1 teaspoon sugar in water, sprinkle yeast over and leave in warm place until frothy. Blend together onion, cheese, butter, salt, eggs and remaining sugar. Mix flours with oats and pour in yeast liquid. Stir in cheese mixture and dill seeds. Knead until smooth. Place dough in warmed, lightly greased bowl and cover with damp cloth or greased plastic wrap and leave in warm place until doubled in size.

Knock back dough and place in 1.5 litre casserole. Cover again and leave to double in size a second time. Bake at 180°C 35 minutes until cooked.

Hint: Dill seeds may be replaced by same amount of caraway seeds or celery seeds.

# Granary Bread

1 teaspoon sugar
30 g fresh yeast
1 cup warm water
¾ cup warm milk
2¾ cups flour
2½ cups wholemeal flour
1 tablespoon salt
1 tablespoon butter
⅔ cup wheatgerm
1 cup cracked wheat
2 tablespoons malt extract
1 tablespoon milk

Dissolve sugar and yeast in the warm water and milk and allow to stand until frothy. Sift flour and salt, shaking any leftover grain into the bowl. Rub in butter and mix in the wheatgerm and cracked wheat. Make a well in the centre of the flour and pour in the yeast mixture. Add malt extract and mix well to form a soft dough. Turn out onto a lightly floured surface and knead until smooth and elastic. Place dough in a lightly greased bowl, cover with a damp cloth or lightly greased plastic wrap and leave in a warm place until doubled in size. Knead dough again and shape into a loaf. Place on a greased loaf pan or on a greased baking sheet cover with a damp cloth or lightly greased plastic wrap and leave in a warm place until doubled in size. Brush the dough with milk and bake at 220°C for 35 minutes.

Hint: Sprinkle cracked wheat over loaf for a crunchy topping.

# Rye Bread

1½ cups plain flour
2 cups rye flour
2 teaspoons salt
1 teaspoon caraway seeds
1 teaspoon sugar
1 cup warm water
2 teaspoons dry yeast
little beaten egg

Place flours, salt and caraway seeds in bowl. Dissolve sugar in warm water, sprinkle over yeast and leave for 10 minutes in warm place until frothy. Make a well in flour, pour in yeast mixture and mix to firm dough. Knead 10 minutes on lightly floured surface. Place dough in warmed, lightly greased bowl and cover with damp cloth or

greased plastic wrap and leave in warm place until doubled in size. Knock back dough, knead again and shape into elongated loaf. Make some diagonal slits along top with sharp knife or razor blade and leave on greased baking tray until doubled in size. Brush loaf with beaten egg and bake at 220°C 30 minutes until cooked.

# Mixed Grain Loaf

30 g fresh yeast
1½ cups warm milk
1 tablespoon sugar
1 tablespoon oil
3 cups wholemeal flour
1 cup plain flour
½ cup soy flour
1 cup bran
½ cup millet meal
1 tablespoon salt

Place yeast in bowl with ½ cup warm milk. Allow to stand until frothy. Add sugar, oil and remaining milk. Place remaining ingredients in a large bowl, stir in liquid and combine to a smooth dough. Cover with a damp cloth or plastic wrap and set in a warm place until dough doubles in size. Turn out onto a board and knead until smooth

and springy. Shape dough into 2 large round loaves and place on baking trays. Cover with a damp cloth or plastic wrap and set in a warm place until dough again doubles in size. Bake at 200°C for 30–40 minutes.

# Rye and Soy Loaf

40 g fresh yeast
125 mL warm milk
1 teaspoon sugar
300 g wholemeal flour
100 g rye flour
100 g soy flour
1 teaspoon salt
125 mL warm water
1 tablespoon oil
extra warm milk

Crumble yeast into warm milk with sugar. Stir to dissolve and set aside until frothy. Place flours and salt in large bowl. Combine warm water with oil and add to flour. Add frothy mixture. Combine to form a smooth dough, adding more milk if dough is too stiff. Cover with a damp cloth or plastic wrap and set in a warm place until dough doubles in size. Turn out

onto a board and knead thoroughly until dough is smooth and springy. Shape into 2 loaves of equal size. Place in oiled bread tins and press dents along centre of loaves with thumb. Cover with a damp cloth or plastic wrap and set aside in a warm place until dough doubles in size. Bake at 200°C for 20 minutes, reduce to 180°C and bake a further 30–40 minutes.

# Cottage Oatmeal Loaf

40 g fresh yeast
15 g sugar
475 mL warm milk
170 g flour
340 g wholemeal flour
1 teaspoon salt
250 g oats
2 teaspoons oil

Place yeast and sugar in a bowl with a little warm milk and allow to stand until frothy. Combine flours and salt in a large bowl. Stir yeast mixture and remaining milk into flour and combine to form a smooth dough. Cover with a damp cloth or plastic wrap and set in a warm place until dough doubles in size.

Work in oil and oats until smooth.

Turn out onto board and knead until uniform and springy. Divide dough into 2 equal portions and place into 18 cm cake tins. Cover with a damp cloth or plastic wrap and set aside in a warm place until the dough has doubled in size. Cut 4 slits in the top of each loaf. Bake at 200°C for 20 minutes, reduce to 180°C and bake a further 15–20 minutes or until loaves are cooked.

Step 1. Pour yeast mixture into flours

Step 2. Work in oil and oats until smooth

Step 3. Form dough into two loaves

Cottage Oatmeal Loaf

# Treacle Bread

¾ cup milk
¼ teaspoon vinegar
1 egg, beaten
¼ cup molasses or treacle
1 tablespoon butter, softened
¼ cup caster sugar
2¼ cups self-raising flour
1 cup wholemeal flour
½ teaspoon salt
½ teaspoon bicarbonate of soda

Mix milk and vinegar together and put aside. Stir egg, molasses, butter and sugar together until well mixed. Sift flours, salt and bicarbonate of soda and combine with egg mixture and milk. Beat thoroughly to smooth batter. Pour into greased 450 g loaf tin and cover tightly with aluminium foil. Place in baking tin containing a little water. Bake at 180°C 1 hour.

# Fruit and Nut Twist

20 g fresh yeast
¾ cup warm milk
2 tablespoons butter
¼ cup sugar
2 cups wholemeal flour
pinch salt
½ teaspoon mixed spice
½ cup mixed dried fruit
½ cup chopped mixed nuts
1 egg

Dissolve yeast with a little sugar in ¼ cup warm milk and allow to stand in a warm place until frothy. Combine remaining milk with butter. Place flour, salt, mixed spice, fruit and nuts and remaining sugar in a bowl. Beat egg into milk and butter mixture. Pour all liquid into bowl and combine to form a smooth dough. Cover with a damp cloth or plastic wrap and set in a warm place until dough doubles in size. Turn out onto floured board and knead thoroughly. Roll dough into a long sausage shape and then loop it into half. Take ends of dough and twist. Place on well-greased oven tray. Cover with a damp cloth and set in a warm place for 20 minutes.

Bake at 220°C for 15–20 minutes. As soon as twist is removed from oven, glaze with a lightly warmed mixture of 1 tablespoon water and 2 tablespoons sugar.

# Date and Orange Raisin Teabread

1 cup chopped dates
⅓ cup raisins
grated rind 1 orange
1 teaspoon sugar
¾ cup warm water
1 tablespoon fresh yeast
3½ cups wholemeal flour
1 tablespoon lard
1 teaspoon salt
2 tablespoons caster sugar
1 egg, beaten with 1 tablespoon water

Dissolve sugar in warm water, crumble in yeast and leave in for 10 minutes in warm place until frothy. Rub lard into flour, add salt, sugar, orange rind, raisins and dates and mix well. Make well in centre, pour in yeast mixture and mix to combine. Knead for 10 minutes until smooth. Place dough in warmed, lightly greased bowl and cover with damp cloth or greased plastic wrap, and leave in warm place until doubled in size. Knock back dough and knead until smooth. Shape to fit 450 g loaf tin or 20 cm cake tin, and leave to rise to top of tin.

Brush loaf with egg and water glaze and bake at 190°C 40–45 minutes.

Fruit and Nut Twist *centre* and Date and Raisin Teabread

# BISCUITS CAKES, AND TREATS

## Date Wholemeal Scones

*½ cup oatmeal*
*½ cup wholemeal flour*
*2¼ cups flour*
*2 teaspoons baking powder*
*100 g butter*
*½ cup brown sugar*
*2 eggs, beaten*
*1 teaspoon mixed spice*
*2 cups chopped dates*
*150 mL milk*
*little milk*

Sift flours and baking powder. Add oatmeal and rub in butter. Add sugar, eggs, spice and dates and combine. Gradually add milk to make a smooth dough. Knead lightly and divide into 20 scones about 6.5 cm in diameter and 1 cm thick. Grease baking tray, arrange scones on it close together and brush lightly with milk. Rest for 10 minutes. Bake at 190°C 15 minutes.
    Makes 20

## Wholemeal Shortbread

*50 g butter*
*⅔ cup wholemeal flour*
*1 tablespoon caster sugar*

Rub butter into flour, add sugar and knead lightly. Roll out on lightly floured board to a 15 cm round. Place on lightly greased baking sheet, flute edges with forefinger and thumb and prick over with fork. Mark into wedges.

Bake at 180°C 25 minutes, until light golden brown. Cool on baking sheet.
    Serves 2–4

Hint: When rolling soft doughs overlap two pieces of greaseproof paper under dough and one piece over top. Lift onto baking sheet or pie dish and slide out the paper.

## Flapjacks

*175 g butter*
*1 tablespoon golden syrup*
*½ cup brown sugar*
*1 cup rolled oats*
*⅛ teaspoon mixed spice*

Melt butter, golden syrup and brown sugar in saucepan. Add rolled oats and mixed spice and combine. Pour into greased 25 × 18 cm baking tray and bake at 190°C for 20 minutes, until golden brown. Cut into 10 fingers while still warm.
    Makes 10

Date Wholemeal Scones

# Oaty Date Squares

1½ cups chopped dates
finely grated rind and juice of 1 orange
100 g butter
¾ cup brown sugar
¾ cup rolled oats
½ cup wholemeal flour

Make up orange juice to 100 mL with water. Cook dates and rind in orange water over low heat until soft and pulpy.

Blend butter and dry ingredients and press half into lightly greased 18 cm square tin. Spread date mixture over, top with remaining oat mixture and press down. Bake at 180°C 35–40 minutes. Cool in tin then cut into 16 squares.
    Makes 16

# Carob Cookies

150 g butter
¾ cup brown sugar
1 egg
¼ cup carob powder
2 cups self raising wholemeal flour
½ cup raisins
½ cup chopped walnuts

Cream butter and sugar, beat in egg then stir in remaining ingredients until well mixed. Roll into walnut-size balls and place on lightly greased baking sheet. Flatten lightly with fingertips or fork.

Bake at 180°C 12–15 minutes. Cool on baking sheet 2–3 minutes then lift on to cake rack to cool completely.
    Makes 45

# Fruity Coconut Bars

½ cup wholemeal flour
1½ teaspoons baking powder
½ teaspoon ground cinnamon
¼ teaspoon ground ginger
⅛ teaspoon ground nutmeg
½ cup brown sugar
½ cup sultanas
½ cup chopped dried apricots
1 cup desiccated coconut
2 eggs, beaten
75 g butter, melted
1 tablespoon milk

Sift flour with baking powder and spices. Combine with sugar, fruit and coconut. Beat in eggs, butter and milk. Spread mixture in greased and lined 18 × 27 cm shallow tin and bake at 180°C 30 minutes. Leave to cool in tin then cut into 16 bars.
    Makes 16

Oaty Date Squares *above*, Carob Cookies and Fruity Coconut Bars

# Mango Filled Roll

½ cup caster sugar
3 eggs, separated
¾ cup flour
2 teaspoons baking powder
2 tablespoons hot milk
2 tablespoons caster sugar and 1
    teaspoon cinnamon combined

## Filling

1 cup mashed mango
1 cup thickened cream
1 tablespoon icing sugar, sifted
1 teaspoon whisky

Grease and paper-line swiss roll tin with greased greaseproof. Sift flour and baking powder in a bowl. Beat egg whites until stiff. Gradually beat in sugar until mixture becomes thick and glossy. Beat in yolks one at a time. Fold in sifted, dry ingredients and hot milk. Pour mixture into tin and smooth the surface. Bake at 220°C for 10 minutes.

Turn cake out onto a sheet of greaseproof paper sprinkled with caster sugar mixture. Roll cake up and allow to cool. Whip cream till thick. Fold in mango, sugar and whisky and chill. Unroll cake and spread with cream.
    Roll up and chill before serving.

Mango Filled Roll

Step 1. Beat egg whites until stiff and gradually beat in sugar

Step 2. Fold in dry ingredients

Step 3. Smooth out mixture with a palette-knife

# Apple-Carrot Muffins

¼ cup grated apple
¼ cup grated carrot
2 tablespoons dried skim milk
1½ teaspoons baking powder
½ teaspoon ground cinnamon
¼ teaspoon ground nutmeg
¼ teaspoon allspice
1¼ cups wholemeal flour
½ cup honey
100 mL safflower or corn oil
2 eggs, beaten
½ teaspoon vanilla essence

Sift milk, baking powder, spices and flour together. Combine honey, oil, eggs and vanilla and stir into dry ingredients. Fold in apple and carrot. Spoon mixture into 14–16 greased deep patty tins and bake at 200°C for 15–20 minutes.
 Makes 14–16 muffins

# Carob Raisin Fudge

1½ cups brown sugar
¼ cup carob powder
100 g butter
170 mL milk
1½ teaspoons vanilla essence
¼ cup raisins

Stir sugar, carob powder, butter and milk over low heat until sugar has dissolved. Bring to boil and boil, without stirring, until mixture reaches 'soft ball' stage or sugar thermometer reaches 110°C. Add vanilla essence and cool to lukewarm.

Beat in raisins and continue to beat until mixture is creamy. Pour into 20 cm square buttered tin and cool. Cut into squares.
 Makes 16

# Peanut Butter Cookies

¾ cup crunchy peanut butter
100 g butter
½ cup brown sugar
¼ cup caster sugar
1 egg
½ teaspoon bicarbonate of soda
½ teaspoon vanilla essence
1 cup wholemeal flour

Cream butter and sugars. Add egg, peanut butter, bicarbonate of soda and vanilla essence and mix well. Blend in flour. Roll mixture into walnut-size balls, place on lightly greased baking sheet and flatten with fingertips or fork.
 Bake at 180°C 10–12 minutes until light brown.
 Makes 35

# Sesame Seed Brittle

1 cup brown sugar
1–1½ cups sesame seeds
1 teaspoon vanilla essence

Stir sugar over low heat until melted. Bring to boil, remove from heat and stir in sesame seeds and vanilla essence. Pour mixture onto greased baking sheet and spread into thin layers. Leave to cool. When cold, break up into small pieces.

# Scones

1 cup plain flour
1 cup wholemeal flour
1 teaspoon cream of tartar
½ teaspoon bicarbonate of soda
½ teaspoon salt
500 g butter
150 mL milk
beaten egg or milk

Sift dry ingredients and rub in butter. Add enough milk to form soft dough. Knead very lightly. Roll or pat out dough to 1.5 cm thickness. Using 5 cm floured cutter, stamp out 10 scones. Place on greased baking sheet, brush tops with egg or milk and bake at 200°C 12–15 minutes. Add sultanas, raisins, mixed dried fruit or grated cheese after butter is rubbed in if desired.
Makes 10

Hint: When cutting out scones do not twist as this prevents scones from rising.

# Parkin

100 g butter
½ cup brown sugar
½ cup golden syrup
2 tablespoons treacle
2¼ cups oatmeal
½ cup plain flour
1 teaspoon baking powder
1 tablespoon ground ginger
1 egg, beaten
1 tablespoon milk

Melt butter, sugar, syrup and treacle over low heat without boiling. Sift dry ingredients and stir in melted ingredients with egg and milk.
Pour into greased and lined 20 cm square cake tin and bake at 140°C 1¾ hours until cooked. Cool in tin.
Makes 8

# Apple Spice Cake

500 g Granny Smith apples, peeled, cored, sliced
4 tablespoons water
½ lemon, juiced
175 g butter
½ cup brown sugar
3½ cups wholemeal flour
1 teaspoon bicarbonate of soda
1 teaspoon ground cinnamon
½ teaspoon ground nutmeg
½ teaspoon ground mace
¼ teaspoon ground cloves
1 cup chopped walnuts
1 cup chopped dates
⅓ cup raisins
3 tablespoons milk

Cook apples over low heat in water and lemon juice until soft. Mash with wooden spoon and leave to cool. Cream butter and sugar. Sift flour with bicarbonate of soda and spices into creamed mixture. Stir in with walnuts, raisins, dates and milk. Spoon into greased 1 kg loaf tin.

## Topping

1 tablespoon brown sugar
¼ cup chopped walnuts
½ teaspoon cinnamon

Combine topping ingredients, sprinkle over cake and bake at 170°C 1¼–1½ hours. Leave to rest for 15 minutes then cool on wire rack.

Hint: When sifting wholegrain flours, tip any leftover grains into mixture, don't throw away.

Step 1. Cook apples in water and lemon juice

Step 2. Cream butter and sugar

Step 3. Stir in dried fruit and nuts

Apple Spice Cake

# Jewish Honey Cake

2½ cups wholemeal flour
2 teaspoons baking powder
2 teaspoons mixed spice
3 eggs
½ cup brown sugar
½ cup honey
3 tablespoons corn oil
2 tablespoons marmalade
½ cup raisins
½ cup chopped almonds
½ cup chopped mixed peel
2 tablespoons orange juice
¼ cup flaked almonds

Sift flour with baking powder and mixed spice. Combine eggs, sugar, honey, oil and marmalade. Mix in dry ingredients with fruits, nuts and orange juice. Pour into greased shallow tin 21 × 16 × 5 cm and sprinkle flaked almonds on top. Bake at 170°C 30 minutes then reduce heat to 150°C and bake further 40–45 minutes until cooked. Cool on wire rack then store in airtight container for 2 days before cutting.

Hint: To test for doneness press fingertips lightly into cake. It should spring back. Cake also recedes slightly from tin when cooked.

Jewish Honey Cake

Step 1. Combine eggs, sugar, oil and marmalade

Step 2. Mix fruit, nuts and orange juice into dry ingredients

# DESSERTS

## Macerated Fruits

2 kg summer fruits, (pears, plums,
  strawberries, raspberries, cherries,
  apricots and peaches)
lemon juice
2 tablespoons honey
600 mL rose wine

Prepare fruit and slice or halve according to size. Sprinkle lemon juice over any likely to brown (such as apples, pears or bananas). Layer fruit in large glass serving dish.

Stir honey into wine and pour over fruit. Leave overnight in refrigerator. Serve with yoghurt or cream.
Serves 12

## Pear and Date Crunch

750 g pears, peeled and cored
250 g dates, halved and stoned
1 tablespoon raw sugar
½ teaspoon ground allspice
150 mL orange juice

### Topping

125 g butter
1¼ cups wholemeal flour
¼ cup raw or brown sugar
½ cup rolled oats
½ teaspoon cinnamon
pinch salt

Cut pears into chunky pieces and place in ovenproof dish with dates, sugar, allspice and orange juice.
Rub butter into flour, stir in sugar, oats, cinnamon and salt. Sprinkle over fruit. Bake at 180°C 40 minutes until pears are soft and topping golden. Serve hot with yoghurt.
Serves 6

## Bread and Butter Pudding

250 g mixed dried fruit
¼ cup orange juice
10 slices wholemeal bread
50 g butter, softened
4 eggs
2 egg yolks
600 mL milk
½ teaspoon vanilla essence
1 tablespoon raw sugar

Soak dried fruit in orange juice for 15 minutes. Spread butter over bread, cut each slice into 4 triangles. Arrange half in a shallow ovenproof dish. Top with fruit and juice and cover with remaining bread.

Beat together the eggs, egg yolks, milk and vanilla and spoon over bread. Sprinkle with sugar. Bake at 180°C 35 minutes, until custard is set and pudding golden brown. Serve hot or cold.
Serves 6

## Atholl Brose

600 mL milk
¼ cup rolled oats
3 tablespoons honey
⅛ teaspoon grated nutmeg
¼ cup whisky

150 mL cream, whipped
1–2 pieces stem ginger in syrup, sliced

Boil milk, sprinkle in oats and simmer 5 minutes, until thick, stirring occasionally. Stir in honey, nutmeg and

whisky and leave to cool.
Fold cream through gently, pour into 2 serving glasses and chill well. Garnish with ginger.
Serves 2

Macerated Fruits

# Plum Flan

## Pastry

*1⅓ cups wholemeal flour*
*100 g butter*
*1 egg yolk*
*a little milk*

Rub butter into flour, add egg yolk and enough milk to form firm dough. Roll out and line 20 cm flan dish. Prick base a few times with fork.

## Filling

*3 egg yolks*
*¼ cup honey*
*300 mL natural yoghurt*
*½ teaspoon powdered cinnamon*
*500 g small plums, halved and stoned*
*½ cup blanched almonds*
*1 tablespoon brown sugar*

Beat yolks with honey, yoghurt and cinnamon. Pour into pastry case.

Arrange plums, cut side down in yoghurt mixture. Bake at 200°C for 35–40 minutes, until custard is set. Sprinkle with nuts and brown sugar and brown under a hot grill.

Serves 6

Step 1. Rub butter into flour, add egg yolk and milk

Step 2. Beat yolks with honey, yoghurt and cinnamon

Step 3. Arrange plums in yoghurt mixture

# Pineapple Calypso

*1 ripe pineapple*
*6 tablespoons chopped fresh mint*
*2 egg whites*
*½ cup caster sugar*

Peel pineapple and cut into quarters lengthwise. Remove hard core from centre of each quarter and cut pineapple into small cubes. Mix with mint and leave in refrigerator overnight.

Spoon pineapple into serving bowl. Beat egg whites until stiff, add half the sugar, beating until dissolved. Beat in remaining sugar until dissolved. Spoon meringue over pineapple and place under griller to brown.

Serves 4–6

# Pears in White Wine

*12 small cooking pears, peeled (leave*
*   stems on)*
*½ cup honey*
*300 mL white wine*
*300 mL water*
*1 lemon*
*1 stick cinnamon*
*4 whole cloves*

Arrange pears in shallow ovenproof dish. Boil honey, wine and water together for 3 minutes and pour over pears. Slice the lemon and add to dish with spices. Cover and bake at 180°C for 1 hour, turning pears occasionally. Leave to cool.

Arrange pears in serving dish, strain juice and pour around pears.

Serves 6

# Baked Apple and Sago Pudding

2 apples, peeled, cored and sliced
¼ cup sago
600 mL milk
3 eggs
2 tablespoons honey
⅛ teaspoon ground nutmeg
⅛ teaspoon ground cloves
2 tablespoons butter

Bring milk and sago to boil and cook 8 minutes. Leave to cool. Beat in eggs, honey and spices. Gently cook apples in butter until soft. Arrange in soufflé dish and fill dish with sago mixture.

Place dish in baking tray half filled with hot water and bake at 180°C 45 minutes. Serve cold.
Serves 4

Step 1. Bring milk and sago to the boil

Step 2. Beat in eggs, honey and spices

Step 3. Gently cook apples in butter

# Apricot Rice Pudding

1 kg apricots
¾ cup short grain rice
1¼ cups water
2½ cups milk
½ cup honey
¼ cup gelatine
2 tablespoons kirsch
150 mL cream

Put rice and half water in saucepan and boil until water has been absorbed. Add milk and simmer 25 minutes. Add ¼ cup honey and gelatine to hot rice and stir well until completely dissolved. Place apricots, remaining water and honey in shallow ovenproof dish and bake at 180°C 20 minutes. Remove from oven and cool. Take 8 apricots from dish and mash in their syrup. Add these to the kirsch and then blend in with the rice. Whip cream and fold into

rice. Place rice in 2 litre jelly or charlotte mould and set in refrigerator for 2 hours until firm.
Turn pudding onto serving dish and decorate with additional apricots.
Serves 6–8

Hint: To turn out moulded dessert, dip mould briefly in hot water and gently tap sides and base before inverting on to serving plate.

# Dried Fruit Crumble

1 cup dried apricots
1 cup dried figs
1 cup pitted prunes
¼ cup raisins
¼ cup currants
¼ cup sugar
1 cup water
¼ cup almonds

2 tablespoons flour
¼ cup desiccated coconut
¼ cup brown sugar
2 tablespoons butter

Soak fruit in enough water to cover for 1 hour. Drain. Place sugar and water in saucepan and bring to the boil. Add fruit and simmer for 30 minutes or until

liquid has been absorbed. Add almonds and place mixture in ovenproof serving dish.
Combine all remaining ingredients and sprinkle over fruit. Bake at 200°C for 15–20 minutes or until top is golden.
Serves 4

Baked Apple and Sago Pudding *above*
and Apricot Rice Pudding

# Sun Glory Pawpaw Pudding

1 cup pawpaw pulp
300 mL milk
⅓ cup semolina
2 tablespoons gelatine
2 tablespoons honey
juice and grated rind 1 lemon
juice and grated rind 1 orange
150 mL cream

## Garnish

1 pawpaw
2 limes or lemons, thinly sliced

Boil milk, stir in semolina and cook 5 minutes. Blend gelatine and honey, stir into hot semolina mixture until dissolved. Flavour with lemon and orange rind and juice, stir in pawpaw and cool.

Whip cream and fold into mixture. Pour into greased 23 cm ring mould. Leave to set in refrigerator for 3–4 hours.

Turn pudding onto serving dish. Scoop out flesh from pawpaw with melon ball cutter and pile into centre. Arrange lime slices around outside, overlapping each other.
Serves 6

Hint: If pawpaw not available, substitute any melon. When grating rind from lemon or orange, do so gently as only the colour is wanted. The white pith is bitter.

Step 1. Boil milk and stir in semolina

Step 2. Blend gelatine and honey

Step 3. Stir in pawpaw

# Kissel

2 cups blackberries
1 lemon, juiced
¼ cup honey
⅛ teaspoon powdered cinnamon
2 cups water
1½ tablespoons arrowroot
1½ tablespoons potato flour
150 mL yoghurt or sour cream

Place blackberries, lemon juice, honey, cinnamon in 1¼ cups water and boil for 5 minutes. Strain through sieve or purée in blender. Return mixture to pan and bring back to boil.

Mix arrowroot and potato flour with remaining water and add to blackberry purée. Cook 4 minutes then pour into individual dishes and cool. Serve topped with yoghurt or sour cream.
Serves 4

# Poached Peaches

4 peaches
¼ cup desiccated coconut
¼ cup ground almonds
½ teaspoon finely grated orange rind
1 egg yolk
2 tablespoons butter
1 cup white wine
1 cinnamon stick

Plunge peaches into boiling water and leave 1 minute. Drain, cover with cold water to cool. Peel, cut in half and remove stones. Place peaches, cut side up, in ovenproof dish. Combine coconut, almonds, orange rind and egg yolk, spoon into peach cavities. Dot with butter. Pour in wine and add cinnamon stick. Cover and bake at 180°C for 20 minutes or until peaches are tender. Remove cinnamon stick and serve warm.
Serves 4–8

# Index

Printed in Singapore